Queen Mother

The Remarkable Life Story of
Rebecca Zirimbuga Musoke

Elizabeth Musoke Mubiru,
M.D., F.A.C.O.G.

Foreword by
Former Prime Minister Joseph G. Mulwanyammuli Ssemwogerere

WESTBOW
PRESS®
A DIVISION OF THOMAS NELSON
& ZONDERVAN

WestBow Press books may be ordered through booksellers or by contacting:

WestBow Press
A Division of Thomas Nelson & Zondervan
1663 Liberty Drive
Bloomington, IN 47403
www.westbowpress.com
1 (866) 928-1240

Because of the dynamic nature of the Internet, any web addresses or links contained in this book may have changed since publication and may no longer be valid. The views expressed in this work are solely those of the author and do not necessarily reflect the views of the publisher, and the publisher hereby disclaims any responsibility for them.

Any people depicted in stock imagery provided by Thinkstock are models, and such images are being used for illustrative purposes only. Certain stock imagery © Thinkstock.

ISBN: 978-1-5127-4153-7 (sc)
ISBN: 978-1-5127-4154-4 (hc)
ISBN: 978-1-5127-4152-0 (e)

Library of Congress Control Number: 2016907453

Print information available on the last page.

WestBow Press rev. date: 8/24/2016

DEDICATED TO THE MEMORY OF OUR PARENTS:

LATIMER KAMYA MUSOKE AND
REBECCA ZIRIMBUGA MUSOKE.

"THE SECRET OF THE WORLD IS LOWLY"

Contents

Foreword

It is indeed a great and imperative idea to remember, in print, a great person in the names of Namasole (Queen Mother) Zirimbuga Rebecca, for her outstanding demeanour, activities and achievements, both overt and covert.

My appointment to the position of Katikkiro (Prime Minister) of the Kingdom of Buganda in 1994 by the Kabaka (King) of Buganda, His Majesty Ronald Muwenda Mutebi II, automatically blessed me with the privileged opportunity to interact directly with Namasole Zirimbuga. She had inherited the role from the late Lady Sarah Namasole Nalule Kabejja. The Namasole occupies a very powerful and enviable position in the Kingdom of Buganda. She is second in command in the hierarchy of the kingdom, presided over by the Kabaka; while the Katikkiro heads the kingdom's government on behalf of the Kabaka.

In order to properly appreciate the delicate role played by Namasole Zirimbuga, it is absolutely necessary to recall that all kingdoms had earlier been abolished in Uganda, and all their properties confiscated and/or vandalised by then Prime Minister of Uganda, Apollo Milton Obote and his Central Government, in 1966. The said properties included Palaces, Kingdom Administrative Headquarters, County and Sub-County offices and residences, Courts of Law, Prisons, Schools, Namasole's homesteads, 9000 Square Miles of land etc, etc.

It is, therefore, against the above background that Buganda Kingdom's restoration, in 1993, must be viewed; and indeed those were the circumstances under which Namasole Zirimbuga shouldered her responsibilities. Although the thrust of the infrastructural, financial, institutional, and mobilisational restoration drives and efforts were carried out by the Katikkiro and his Cabinet on behalf of the Kabaka, much of the salient royal, cultural and traditional underpinnings were to be principally driven, directed and finalised by Namasole Zirimbuga and the clan leaders.

Generally speaking, Namasole Zirimbuga was viewed publicly as an iron lady with an outward no-nonsense attitude; but deep inside her, she was a mother-figure. She exuded a very deep love for her Kabaka and her culture, and she was extremely kind at heart and very generous to the kingdom. She made personal sacrifices in order to carry out her duties to the kingdom!! All these unique attributes came in handy as she went about executing her very delicate responsibilities. It is no wonder that she registered the resultant success and stability in the immediate and wider royal family.

This is not to say that her job was without challenges. Far from it. The kingdom she was nursing was only freshly restored, the Kabaka had been living away in exile, she was working with a brand new Katikkiro, the first Catholic, and operating in an environment where much of the Kiganda culture, customs and traditions had for a long time been quietly ostracised and largely forgotten; and most importantly, she was operating in a kingdom without sufficient money nor with powers to mobilise funds through taxation.

The Katikkiro, together with his team, and under the guidance of the Kabaka struggled to establish means of income and an improved working environment by setting up the Buganda Land Board, the CBS Radio, the Buganda Cultural and Development Foundation (BUCADEF), the Buganda Investment and Commercial Undertaking Limited (BICUL) and the Kabaka's Education Fund. We fully furnished the hitherto empty Bulange Administrative Headquarters at Mengo; reconstructed Kabaka's palaces; repaired Kasubi Tombs and other Cultural Sites; and secured land at Bumbu in Wakiso District for Namasole Zirimbuga's Palace. It is painful that she passed away before the full construction was completed for her official occupation.

On a personal level, Namasole Zirimbuga treated me and loved me like her son; and by extension, treated and loved my mother, the late Mrs. Bernadeth Nantale Mulwanya, like her sister. Each time my mother came to Mengo to buy Certificates for Voluntary Contribution to the kingdom, the Namasole would spare time to be in attendance, and they would dine together for lunch. They would visit each other regularly. And when my mother passed away, Namasole Zirimbuga attended the Church Funeral Service at Lubaga Cathedral, despite her poor health at the time. I miss her greatly.

History will definitely view Namasole Zirimbuga as a great, respectable and selfless lady, who offered her services to her Kabaka and to the kingdom without any reservations whatsoever. She was understanding, accommodative, generous and approachable. She was hardworking, dedicated and exemplary, both in her official duties and in her private life and household. Namasole Zirimbuga loved her King; she loved the Royal Family; she loved Buganda, she loved Uganda, she loved people generally, and she loved her God.

I commend her outstanding demeanour, and may her soul rest in eternal peace.

J. G. MULWANYAMMULI SSEMWOGERERE
Former Katikkiro (Prime Minister)
of Buganda Kingdom.
Bulange- Mengo.

Introduction

They say some are born to greatness, some earn it and some have it thrust upon them. Rebecca had it dropped on her like a ton of bricks, against the wishes of herself *and* her father. She had been content to be the wife of a brilliant man and the mother of seven lively children whom she adored and who adored her. She thought her life would continue the same way indefinitely, but she learnt that with every corner you turn in life, there might be another surprise waiting for you.

Rebecca was born into a life of privilege in an age-old African kingdom steeped in tradition. Times had changed since the kingdom had been swallowed up by the British Empire in the late 1800s, and later absorbed into a newly independent African country in the early 1960s. The kingdom strove to maintain its identity through the turbulence of political coups and savage regimes bent on annihilating it. Finally, the kingdom fell to its haters and the king was exiled for life. As Rebecca guided her young family through the perilous times, she held onto her faith that someday the kingdom would be restored and life would return to 'normal'.

Rebecca believed in a God who answered her prayers and that 'where there's a will, there's a way.' She was surrounded by the people she loved and was busy with her demanding work. Although she had grown up with them, Rebecca had little time in her busy life to interact closely with her cousins who had married into the kingdom's royal family. Then one of Rebecca's cousins passed away. They were holding her late cousin's last funeral rites when she heard her name being whispered back and forth as the heir to the **queen mother.** She would never forget that day. The new responsibility could change her life forever!

Since the kingdom had been abolished seven years earlier in a military coup, Rebecca managed to avoid the zealous homage of those who would have recognised her for a while. But times *did* change and after many years of bloodshed, sweat and tears, the kingdom was restored. Elated as she was, Rebecca did not relish the thought of becoming famous. She preferred the comfort of immediate family and close friends to public acclaim. But when duty called, Rebecca set her own desires aside and rose to the challenge of becoming: **The Mother of the Kingdom of Buganda (Namasole)!**

This is the story of her life; a life that triumphed over perilous times, personal tragedy and painful illness to see her family grow and thrive while nurturing the restoration of the kingdom. The narrative is taken from her timeless stories, her audio tapes and her diaries and is supplemented by the loving memories of her children and grandchildren. Finally, it includes the many tributes from family and friends written to the memory of Rebecca Zirimbuga Musoke, nee Kisosonkole.

Chapter One

Childhoood

Times have changed since the 'colonial days' into which Rebecca was born on the 19th of February, 1932. She was the only daughter of her parents for a long time; a fact she had often lamented. One day, she asked her mother, "How come every time you go to hospital they give you a boy baby?"

"Because that's what God wants," her mother replied calmly.

At first she used to run to her father every time one of her brothers hit her. One day, her father said to her, "Becca, you can't keep running away the rest of your life; you must learn to fight back." So she learnt to play and fight with her five brothers; she had to show those boys she could do whatever they did. Yes, she could climb trees, kick a football and run faster than most of them, but two things had defeated her: that pesky 'riding a bicycle' thing and the knack of throwing at a target. While her brothers could throw rocks at the ripe mangos and knock them off the trees, she had to learn to climb; so she did. Even then, she was a determined little person. She would have learnt to ride a bicycle too, but her brothers told her that in order to learn, she had to take at least one bad fall. She was scared of that.

Mother had to continually remind Rebecca that she was a girl and should not act like the boys. Her father didn't have to remind her. She was Daddy's little girl; always tagging along with him whenever she had the chance to. He would take her along with him when he was surveying the land and checking on his tenants. They would take long walks together in the woods in what seemed like an exciting wilderness experience. She could talk to her father about anything, and she thought that he shared deep secrets with her, too. He thoroughly spoilt her, but that didn't stop Rebecca from getting in trouble. Like the time they were playing on their father's scooter and it fell on their baby brother. His screams brought their mother running to the scene of the 'crime'. He was all right, but they all got a sound spanking for it. For some reason, Rebecca always got the soundest one. Her father always seemed to suspect that she was the ringleader, even though she wasn't the eldest.

There was Adolphus (Dolphe), her older brother; then Josephus (Joe), who came after her; then Arnold (Spero), then Myers, then Michael (Tempora) – all before baby sister Damallie showed up. She had given up praying for a sister by then, but she had plenty of girl cousins to make up for it. There were Sarah and Damali, Uncle Christopher's daughters; Christine and Jesse, Auntie Tolofaina's daughters and Betty and Nancy, Auntie Marjorie's daughters. When Rebecca was little, her father, Kupliano Lufo Bisase Kisosonkole, was a schoolteacher at the prestigious King's College Budo, where he taught English. Her mother, Damali Najjuma Bisase Kisosonkole, was an industrious homemaker who kept an immaculate home. Their numerous aunts and uncles doted on them all. Every month, her father's family would get together at one or the other of their homes. Their home in Budo was a particular favourite because of mother's talents. She cooked and baked and sewed all their clothes, even the boys' shirts and shorts. She also had a very productive vegetable garden whose produce they often ate from. Rebecca could only hope to be as industrious as her mother when *she* grew up.

Luganda was Rebecca's first language. She first learnt English from her own father. He would teach her and her brothers nursery rhymes and read them bedtime stories. Her earliest memories of learning to read and write in school were painful ones. If you formed a letter incorrectly, the teacher, Mr. Samuel Nkata, would twist your ear. He would say, "That's how the letter feels when you write it the wrong way." One day, she and Dolphe were walking to school when they were chased by a dog. Rebecca must have run faster than her brother, because the next thing she knew, he had fallen down. Rebecca looked down at her brother. He wasn't moving and didn't respond when she called his name. Thankfully, some grown-ups who had been watching came running over and picked him up. Rebecca went on to school by herself. She sat down in class but said nothing to the teacher.

The next day the teacher asked her, "Rebecca, where is your brother?"

"He's at home," she replied.

"What happened to him?" the teacher asked. That's when Rebecca explained that her brother had fallen down and had to be carried home. She got in trouble with the teacher because she hadn't reported the incident, but couldn't figure out why she had to be punished. She had really been afraid that her brother had been seriously injured, but her mother reassured her that he was going to be all right.

Rebecca didn't remember being spanked very often by her mother. Whenever she *was* spanked though, Josephus would cry and refuse to eat his supper. They had nicknamed him 'Tarzan' because when he cried, he sounded just like Tarzan from the movie '*Tarzan of the Apes*'. He was closer to Rebecca than her other brothers and would often stick up for her. One occasion she remembered very well was when they left baby Myers playing near the sewing machine. He managed to get his finger stuck under the needle of the sewing machine. Why did he have to get himself caught up in everything, mischievous little chap? On another occasion, they heard their Aunt Alex tell their mother that the manservant Job resembled their dog, Kagezi. Rebecca and her brother Dolphe thought that was funny and repeated it. Mother didn't think it was so funny and shut them in their room. Well, that was just an opportunity for them to shout what they had heard out through the window: "Job, you look like the dog, Kagezi!" Were they in trouble!

One day, Rebecca and her brothers stayed out late playing board games and came home to find all the doors of the house locked. They knew they were in trouble and were afraid to knock on any of the doors and wake up their parents. After weighing their options, they ended up sleeping on the floor of the storeroom adjacent to the front veranda. In the morning, the others nominated Rebecca to knock on the front door. Their father opened the door. He told her, "Go inside, take a bath and then pack up your things." Rebecca was too scared to ask him why.

She went inside and asked her mother, "What did Daddy mean?"

Her mother responded, "What did he say?" Rebecca repeated her father's words.

"Do whatever your father told you to do," her mother said. Their father drove them all to their grandfather's house for the holidays. Looking back, Rebecca could not remember a single incident regarding their children in which her parents had disagreed. Even when it seemed that they had not had time to discuss it, they were always of one mind regarding discipline. Rebecca had to quickly learn to be a more responsible older sister.

Rebecca took the devoted love between her parents for granted. She took it for granted that every Sunday the whole family was in church; that every evening before dinner the family would read the Bible and pray together. Regular meals at the table with the whole family, and anyone else who happened to drop in, were taken for granted, too. Rebecca's life was full of adventure as well. She enjoyed the beauty of the interlacustrine lands they owned; the evergreen, undulating hills off the shores of Lake Victoria covered with lush vegetation and fruit trees that could be picked all year round; the noise of farm animals that heralded them from dawn till dusk; the long sunny days that made you want to skip school and the rainy seasons that always lasted too long.

Rebecca's father owned several acres of vanilla orchards. He would often take her and her brothers out to the farm during harvest season. There he would leave them with the labourers, ostensibly to help with the harvesting and learn the value of hard work. However, the children had figured out that they could easily hide among the vines playing and chewing sugar cane until it was almost time to go home. Then they would quickly gather enough beans in their baskets to convince their father that they had been hard at work all day. That was the fertile land that Sir Winston Churchill had named 'The Pearl of Africa'.

Chapter Two

History

Those were the 'good old days' when the British colonialists were still in power, but the Kabaka (King) of Buganda and his government still wielded considerable power. Father was a good storyteller. He would sit his children down and teach them the history of the family, as well as the history of the Kingdom of Buganda. The Buganda Kingdom is said to have been in existence for at least 700 years when the European explorers 'discovered' it in the mid-1800s. The reigning Kabaka (30th in an unbroken line of succession), Mutesa I (1856-1884), was open-minded. The banana culture (named because of the staple food of the Baganda) does not permit one to be rude to elders or visitors. About twenty years earlier, his father, Kabaka Ssuuna II (1832-1856) had welcomed the Arab traders and their Islamic religion, and now Kabaka Mutesa I invited Her Majesty (Queen Victoria of England) to send Christian missionaries. They arrived between 1875 and 1877. By this time, slavery had already been abolished in the Western world, and the Europeans appeared to want nothing more than to trade and enrich the lives of the 'natives' with their religion and their knowledge.

Kabaka Mwanga II succeeded his father on his death in 1884. The British had firmly established themselves in East

Africa by then and were attempting to colonise the whole region on behalf of Her Majesty, the Queen of England. The 'Scramble for Africa' that resulted in the Berlin Conference of 1884-85 awarded Buganda to the British as part of British East Africa (Kenya and Uganda). Kabaka Mwanga became suspicious of the colonialists' motives; their governance was beginning to interfere with his authority over his subjects as some converted to Christianity, others to Islam. He alternately cooperated with, and then rebelled against the British as they attempted to co-opt his kingdom into what they later called the 'Protectorate of Uganda.' At one point, he had to fight against one of his own brothers to reclaim his throne. Finally, in 1899, he and the Omukama (King) of the neighbouring Bunyoro Kingdom were banished from their kingdoms to the islands of Seychelles by the British governor. Kabaka Mwanga died in exile in the year 1903, on the very same island to which he had been banished.[1]

Rebecca's grandparents on both sides of the family had converted to Christianity when the Christian missionaries came. Although they were living in a culture steeped in tradition, they had also embraced the Western culture. Her paternal grandfather's given name was Kungu, but when he became a Christian, he renamed himself Tefiro *Kisosonkole (empty shell)*, saying, "If a man does not have the Spirit of God in him, he is just an empty shell." Kisosonkole had distinguished himself in his service to Kabaka Mwanga II and steadily risen through the ranks of the chiefs. It was from this position that he and the Regents appointed by the British Colonialists: Apollo Kaggwa, Stanislas Mugwanya and Zakaria Kisingiri, skilfully guided the kingdom through the turbulent times, until the deposed king's infant son, Daudi Chwa, came of age and took over the reins of the kingdom in 1914.

Tefiro Kisosonkole and his wife lost their first two children in infancy. Rebecca's father, born in 1899, was the first child who survived infancy and they named him Kupliano Bisase.

Bisase was only a few years younger than the boy king, Daudi Chwa, and Kisosonkole was elected the young king's guardian from 1900 until 1914. Rebecca often heard the story told that when the Kabaka was going to England to attend the coronation of King George V in 1911, he was told that he didn't need to take Kisosonkole with him because he didn't speak English. The boy king's reply was, "If he doesn't go, I'm not going!" Eventually, the Kabaka appointed Tefiro Kisosonkole Prime Minister of the kingdom from 1927 until 1929.

Kisosonkole was a favourite in the palace courts, but he became very ill during his second year as Prime Minister and was advised to step down. It was no wonder; he had lost his beloved wife, Damali Nalule, and she had left him with six children: two boys and four girls, two of whom were quite young. The Kabaka advised him to remarry, which he did. His second wife, Drusilla, bore him several children in his old age, too. Kabaka Chwa II and his guardian, Kisosonkole, were so close that they died within three months of each other, even though separated by decades in age.

Rebecca wasn't aware of it growing up, but since her grandfather had once been Prime Minister, they were part of a privileged class. Rebecca's father had himself travelled to England in 1925. It was a three-month journey by ship, and by the time he returned three years later, he had lost his beloved mother. Studying in England gave Kupliano a global sense of the world which he wanted all his children to learn, and he encouraged them to leave home early. He had wanted to marry Rebecca's mother, Damali Najjuma, before he went and take her with him. Her father, the treasurer in Kabaka Chwa's government, had agreed, but his own father refused. He said, "How could you even consider taking our friend's precious young daughter to a foreign land?" Instead, Damali went from Gayaza High School to King's College Budo, the first female 'admitted' to the boy's school. Gayaza High School had been started by Anglican Church missionaries in 1905 to educate the daughters of chiefs in the Buganda Kingdom. King's College Budo was started by missionaries the following year to educate the *sons* of the same said chiefs.

Rebecca's mother went to live with a Mr. and Mrs. Robinson (the school nurse) at Budo so that she could learn 'proper' English manners while she waited for her fiancé to return from England. She had to learn British etiquette if she was one day going to accompany the queen to England as a lady-in-waiting. Somehow, they were going to have to merge British royal customs with the royal customs of Buganda. Damali learnt her English etiquette very well. After she and Kupliano got married on his return in 1928, she often had to entertain important visitors. The way that she prepared and served the tea was so typically English, everyone commented on it. She would arrange a small table for each guest, draped with white table linen and a matching serviette. Each table was set with a cup, saucer and spoon, as well as a small teapot, milk jug and sugar bowl. She would then serve freshly baked cake, scones or sandwiches. She was very particular: the slices of bread for the sandwiches had to be cut to a certain width and the edges neatly trimmed. She didn't say very much when the guests arrived, but she made sure they were well catered for. Rebecca told herself that she wanted to learn to be a great hostess herself so that she could pass that on to her daughters.

In 1937, Rebecca's mother travelled to South Africa to study Home Economics. She was away for almost two years and Rebecca missed her terribly. Baby Arnold had been left with their maternal grandmother, Rebecca Zirimbuga. The three older children stayed at home with their father. It was during this time that this grandmother, for whom Rebecca had been named, passed away. Rebecca remembered their father taking them to visit her shortly before she died.

Dolphe whispered to Rebecca, "Is that really her?"

Rebecca replied, "I don't know. The voice is hers, but this lady is so thin; I don't think it's her."

That was the first funeral the children ever attended, but they were not permitted to view the body. Their father told them that if they wanted to remember the deceased person, they should take flowers to her gravesite. When she didn't see her grandmother anymore, Rebecca concluded that's what death meant: you never saw the person again. Death became a fearful thing to the little girl.

Sadly, Cousins Sarah, Damali and Chrispin lost their mother, Victoria, while Rebecca's mother was in South Africa. It was a devastating time in the family. Her husband, Uncle Christopher Sekuuma, was inconsolable. The two brothers were very close and although they were still young, Rebecca's father admonished her and her brothers to comfort their older cousins. Rebecca and her cousin Chrispin were only five years old, but Rebecca never forgot her Aunt Victoria. There was a particular flower that always brought her to her mind. Uncle Christopher left for South Africa the following year, probably to recuperate from his loss. This was long before apartheid became an official government policy and members of the British Commonwealth regularly travelled to South Africa. To their surprise, Uncle Christopher returned a year later with a new South African bride. It was the talk of the town! Rebecca's father invited her uncle and his new bride to live in their home while he rebuilt his own house. Rebecca learnt that her new aunt didn't speak any Luganda, only English. It was a major adjustment for her cousins, but they did their best to make them all feel at home.

Rebecca was ten years old when she lost one of her paternal grand aunts. She was named her heir and fetched from school to attend the last funeral rites. It is customary for all adults, male and female, to have an heir of the same gender named after them. There may not be any property for them to inherit, but depending on the role that was held by the deceased in society, there may be cultural duties and family responsibilities to be taken over. Rebecca inherited a suitcase full of clothes from the old lady. She didn't want to wear any of her dead grand aunt's clothes, though! What if she died too?

Rebecca's mother had taught her how to sew and knit very early. Her mother made it clear that since they were blessed with so much, it was their responsibility to share with others. Together they would visit old widows around the village, taking them food and offering to mend their clothes. Rebecca started giving the clothes she had inherited away to the old widows on the visiting circuit, one by one. By the time her mother realised what was going on, there was only one garment left in the suitcase. Her mother cut up the garment into smaller pieces and made her embroider them as little gifts to give away.

Chapter Three

School Days

Two life-changing events occurred in her life before Rebecca became a teenager. First, her beloved paternal grandfather, Tefiro Kisosonkole, died. The year was 1940. His death instantly changed the family dynamics. Being the eldest son, Rebecca's father was named the heir; but Grandfather Tefiro had not clearly divided his estate among his offspring. She painfully watched as the family was divided into two camps: one on her father's side and the other on her Uncle Christopher's. They argued over the property rights between themselves and the young widow that he had left behind with her six children. No amount of negotiation could bring the matter to a satisfactory conclusion for any involved. The result was that they eventually had to move out of their home in Kireka, which Rebecca's parents had built themselves, to their grandfather's house in Mulawa.

There began a family feud that Rebecca lamented over for a lifetime. She remembered how her parents had lovingly planned and built their first house at Kireka. She and her brothers had helped carry the stones up the hill for the house and the water tank. Her mother had designed and planted a beautiful garden around the house. The house was situated at the very top of the hill with a breath-taking view of Lake Victoria. She and her brothers loved to watch the planes as they approached for their landing on the water at Entebbe Airport.

The second event was the strike of the African teachers at King's College Budo in 1942. The teachers had had a disagreement with the headmaster, Mr. Dennis Herbert. They wrote to the British Board of Governors demanding that the headmaster be removed or they would quit. Their demands were met with paternalistic sarcasm and the school closed down for a while. Kabaka Chwa II had died in 1939, but his son, Edward Mutesa, was not crowned king until 1942 when he turned 18. The coronation had had to be approved by the British government. It took place at the traditional coronation site, Naggalabi on Buddo hill, while Rebecca and her family were still living there. Due to the strike, there was no school, so Rebecca and her brothers watched the coronation with fascination. She had no idea, then, what the next coronation would signify to her. A short time later, all the teachers who had gone on strike were summarily dismissed from the school, including her father. Her mother always said she had warned Kupliano not to join the strike of 1942. Everyone knew he was being groomed to be the first African headmaster of the school. Right or wrong, Rebecca had to leave Budo Primary school and transfer to a new school.

It was hard for Rebecca to concentrate on her schooling after the transfer from Budo. The African teachers from Budo who had been dismissed had been like a family; celebrating all their children's birthdays together every three months. They started a new school, Aggrey Memorial Primary School, at the home of former Prime Minister Sir Apollo Kaggwa. Many families brought their children to the new school. They had heard that all the best teachers from Budo were there. However, it wasn't long before school inspectors came by and told them that the location of the new school was illegal and that they had to move. Rebecca and Dolphe had to start attending classes with children of different ages in the front room of someone's home on Rubaga Road.

Rebecca's family had briefly moved to Mengo and then on to their house at Kireka. After school, the children would have lunch at their Aunt Tolofaina's (Try's) house nearby, and then wait for their father to pick them up in the car he had inherited from his father. It was nice to have a car of their own. However, you couldn't count on Daddy not to stop on the road if he saw an old couple or a pregnant woman walking. Then he would tell Rebecca and the boys to get out and walk so that he could give 'those more deserving' a ride.

Aggrey School was later built near the Kabaka's lake in Mengo. Rebecca's father donated some of his land for the rest of the school grounds. On many occasions, Rebecca and her brothers still had to walk to school and sometimes they were late. They decided they didn't like spending afternoons at their aunt's house. One day, instead of going there, they decided to walk the eight miles home to Kireka through Nakawa and Kinawataka. They joked and laughed and chased each other all the way, so it didn't seem far at all. Mother opened the door to see those naughty children standing there with guilty looks on their faces. Their excuse that their aunt hadn't been home wasn't believed by either of their parents; but both wisely knew there must be a good reason why the children had walked all the way home.

Mother was expecting a baby and Rebecca was hoping and praying fervently for a baby sister. Once again, she was disappointed when she was shown a new baby brother and she tried hard to hide her disappointment. It wasn't long after that the family had to move again. The clan elders instructed her father to move his family from Kireka to their grandfather's house at Mulawa, five miles away, in order to settle the family dispute. It was especially difficult for their mother who, with a new baby, had to give up her house and beautiful garden. Rebecca was kept busy helping her mother with the baby and trying to keep up with her schoolwork. Their father decided there and then that their home in Mulawa was too far away from the school and moved Rebecca and her brothers into town. He moved them into a room in the large house their grandfather had built on Kabaka Anjagala Road in Mengo.

The road on which their grandfather had built his house in town was a beautiful, tree-lined street that led up to the Kabaka's palace. Mengo is the seat of government of the entire Kingdom of Buganda. The parliament (lukiiko) building was later built on the other end of that very street, facing the palace. In the middle was placed a roundabout with a gate. The gate is only opened for the king to pass through; all commoners still have to go around it. Since their parents had remained in their Mulawa home with the two youngest children, Myers and Tempora, Rebecca and her three brothers were left in the charge of a manservant.

Daudi, the manservant, was a very strict but loyal member of the household. School didn't start until 8:30 a.m. and it was only 15 minutes away, but he insisted that the children had to be out of the house by 8:00 o'clock. After school, he kept track of the children by writing down when they left home, where they were going and what time they returned. If you came home a minute after 7:00 p.m., you weren't allowed to eat supper with your siblings. You were served your supper when everyone else had finished. Rebecca had to help with the washing and ironing and cleaning of the house. Her brothers had to fetch water from the stream at the bottom of the hill. The boys had their bicycles but Rebecca didn't, of course. She had never learnt to ride one.

There were several incidents of unrest during Rebecca's school days. One year, while they were still living in Kireka, there was a train derailment in which several people were killed. Another year, the people went on strike and refused to allow any food into the city. All vehicles carrying edibles from the east on Jinja road were stopped at Kireka and their contents spilled. The stench was terrible for weeks. In 1945, there was disagreement between the people and their lukiiko (parliament), and the Prime Minister, Martin Luther Nsibirwa, was assassinated. Despite the upheaval, Rebecca eventually made it back to King's College Budo at the junior level. It was 1946 and it was her first time in a boarding school.

At fourteen, Rebecca was still a shy, quiet, but determined young teenager. Boarding school was daunting, however. The older girls, some of whom were her own cousins, seemed so tall and self-assured. She was living in Ssabaganzi dormitory, but later moved to a cottage she shared with eight other girls. There were so many rules and regulations: you had to dress and make your bed one specific way; you could only wash and iron on Fridays; there was no leaving the school grounds.

Rebecca's parents visited her regularly and brought her milk to drink. Upon their marriage, her maternal grandfather had given her parents a number of dairy cows, saying, "I want to make sure that my grandchildren have milk to drink every day." And they did; boarding school wasn't going to change that. Famine broke out in the year 1949 and the school introduced 'akawunga' (maize meal) for the first time. The school cafeteria would serve akawunga for lunch and Irish potatoes for supper. The aromas of the two meals became forever linked in Rebecca's olfactory memory.

Her parents bought Rebecca a charcoal iron. Even when she shared it with others, she became the envy of older girls. They would use the iron all day before giving it back to her. By the time she got the iron back one Friday, it was time for 'lights out'. She was trying to iron by the light of a dimmed hurricane lamp when it fell on her right arm. Rebecca couldn't tell the house mother what she had been doing when the lamp hit her. She never forgot the excruciating pain of recovery from that burn; trips to the school nurse every day to have the bandages changed. The scar on her arm would always remind her.

Rebecca did learn to swim while she was in boarding school at Budo. That became one of her favourite activities. One day, she was reported for breaking a school rule: a group of girls had left the school grounds and Rebecca was named among them. A spot roll call had been called and all the girls who missed it were to be suspended. Rebecca was devastated. What would her father say? Rebecca wouldn't have dreamt of leaving the school grounds; she was too scared of the world out there. She knew it must have been one of her cousins; people often couldn't tell them apart. She tried in vain to declare her innocence; tearfully telling the house mother that she had been at the swimming pool. Then she went back to her cubicle, knelt down and prayed.

They were brought before the school council, but Rebecca wasn't about to be a telltale. The culprits had been identified by the school cook. The cook said, "I'm not sure which of these two girls is the culprit, but the one who broke the rule can whistle and the other one cannot." The two cousins were separated and each asked to whistle; something Rebecca never could do 'til the day she died. She was relieved to be exonerated, but suspected that her cousin probably never knew why.

Boarding schools can be cruel places for the uninitiated and Rebecca learnt the hard way. Being accused of being a telltale meant being ostracised and sometimes the butt of cruel jokes. Sometimes she would come back to her bed and find it had been doused with water. Her friend Sarah Sebaana would encourage her. When she failed her secondary school entrance examinations a second time and had to leave school, she never forgot the kindness of her friend, Gladys Nsibirwa. She left her a note in her bed which said, "You've had a difficult year here, but I can see that you've persevered; if you continue, God will reward you." She and Gladys had become firm friends after lightning struck the school one day and killed Gladys's sister. Whenever there was a thunderstorm marked with intense lightning, she would run to Rebecca's bed and they would ride out the storm together. Rebecca was afraid of the lightning, too, although she couldn't explain to her friend why.

As she packed her things, Rebecca thought to herself, 'Well, maybe, I'm just not that bright.' What she didn't know then, was that a staff member who particularly disliked her parents was determined that Rebecca would never pass her exams. She was excited, though, because her mother had just had another baby. The longed-for baby sister had finally arrived!

Chapter Four

Study Abroad

Rebecca's parents wouldn't let her be discouraged and continued to encourage her towards a career. They were doing their best to open doors for her both socially and academically. However, when her older cousins came of age and started visiting the palace, Rebecca's parents kept her away. Rebecca wasn't curious about life in the palace, though; she was too busy trying to choose between a career and becoming the wife of a handsome young doctor who had captured her heart.

Career choices for women were still limited in those days: nurse, teacher, social worker. Rebecca's parents arranged for her to take a six-month course in social work, in Kenya. Her two younger brothers, Joe and Arnold, had already been sent off to school in Egypt. Rebecca travelled to Nairobi by train for the first time. Sitting by her father, she could enjoy the passing scenery without interruption. It was exciting to cross the Nile River and see the falls. That was before Owen Falls Dam was built. She noticed when the rolling, tree-smothered hills flattened out into grassy plains. The trees were more scattered and had fewer leaves. When the train took the steep descent into the rift valley, it was frightening. They said there had once been man-eating lions in the valley that the early European explorers had had to overcome. Rebecca craned her neck in vain to see if she could see any of these monsters. She would never forget the breath-taking beauty she witnessed as they climbed the escarpment out of the rift valley. At one point, it almost seemed like the train was suspended in the air. How could anyone doubt the power of a God who could create such an awesome panorama?

Rebecca started her social work studies at the British Council's school in Kabete. Although she was shy, she was naturally drawn to people and loved to interview them and learn each of their stories. The students were taken to visit the farm of a British settler in the rift valley. There, Rebecca saw a house run with electricity for the first time. Lady Allen Cole was a widow who owned 1,000 head of cattle and had many Kenyan farm hands. The students joined the farmhands before sunrise to help with the milking and then returned for breakfast at 10:00 a.m. The farm hands were allowed to own some of their own sheep, but Rebecca was surprised to find out that the maximum they were allowed to own was eight. When their animals bore young and exceeded eight, they had to sell some of them off. They were not allowed to own any cows in their flock, however. Rebecca thought that was unfair. She was already learning to be a voice for the underprivileged.

There were many dynamic Kenyans in Rebecca's class, including Tom Mboya, who later became a politician and statesman. He liked to compare her life in Uganda with theirs in Kenya. One day he said to her, "The difference between Uganda and Kenya is that we have a colour bar, whereas you have a class bar." He continued, "We cannot sit in first class on the train because of our colour; for you, it's your money that determines whether you sit in first class or third class." He pointed out that in Kenya they had signs over some businesses that read, 'No Africans allowed' whereas Ugandans could go to any cinema hall, hotel or restaurant. The year was 1950.

Upon her return to Uganda, Rebecca's parents encouraged her to pursue a degree in social work at the Delphi School of Social Work, a Christian school in India.

Rebecca asked her father, "Daddy, will I manage life in India?"

Her father reassured her: "Yes, you will Becca; remember, I've been to India." Her father had attended the 1938 Third International Mission Conference held in Tambaram, near Madras, India, which later became the World Council of Churches.

Her parents bought Rebecca an airline ticket on All India Airlines. She and her father travelled by train to Nairobi where she was going to board the plane to India. While they were there, they stayed at the home of the Indian High Commissioner to East Africa, Apa Pant. The next day, she boarded the plane with the nephew of the High Commissioner's wife, who was a pilot. He had been tipped off by her father that Rebecca loved planes and he asked her if she wanted to see inside the cockpit. "Of course!" she said. Rebecca got to sit in the pilot's seat for ten minutes while he showed her the controls! She couldn't help thinking, 'What if instead of social work she was going to study to be a pilot?'

Rebecca was experiencing many new and exciting things for the first time. She left East Africa with the words of her father echoing in her heart, "Becca, whatever you have to endure, be strong; that's the only way you will reach your goal." She fell asleep still thinking about what that would mean while she was in India. Thankfully, the plane ride was uneventful and they landed safely in New Delhi. She was met at the airport and driven to the school principal's home. It was already getting dark, so she could not see much of the city, but she could hear, smell and almost taste the sounds of the city that would be her home for the next year. The school principal's name was Miss Moses. Miss Moses welcomed her and told her there were two other foreign female students in the school. There was a second year student from Indonesia and a first year student, like her, from Burma. Rebecca and Mary from Burma became the best of friends. They were later 'adopted' by an older Indian student whom they fondly named 'grandma'.

It took a while for Rebecca to fall asleep that first night; she was exhausted but still excited. The next morning, she woke up with sunlight flooding the room. She looked at her watch; it said it was only 4:00 a.m. It was daylight, so her watch must have stopped. Her two roommates were fast asleep, but everyone else must be up! Rebecca got out of bed, went out and took her bath, then came back to the room. By the time her roommates woke up an hour later, Rebecca was sitting on her bed reading her Bible. They looked at her in astonishment. "Why are you up so early?"

"We always wake up this early at home, " she replied. She didn't want to admit that she had forgotten to reset her watch and the early sunrise had fooled her.

Rebecca never forgot her experience in India. She had arrived in July. In the summer time, it was so hot that the students would take their mattresses onto the roof of the dormitory and sleep there. No wonder that the rooftops had to be flat. She had never seen poverty to the point where people slept in ditches or made their living by begging. The people seemed so different and saw her, an educated black woman, as an oddity. Yet they were also curiously the same. Their caste system was even more brutal than the class system she had been raised in. In Buganda, you were either 'omulangira' (royalty), 'omwana w'omwami' (the child of landed gentry) or 'omukopi' (a commoner). She was the child of landed gentry. However, here she was as dark as the 'Untouchables' who were considered the lowest class in India. Sometimes the children would come up to her and rub her arm to see if the colour would rub off. Or sneak a hand out to touch her hair and see what it felt like. On the train, she rode in the women's coach, but after being spat at and thrown off the train a couple of times as an 'Untouchable', she changed her travelling style. If she wasn't with her protective schoolmates on a field trip, Rebecca would wear trousers so she could ride in the men's coach.

The school principal and teachers were always very kind to Rebecca and the other foreign students. They were often invited over for tea and taken around the city sightseeing. Rebecca got to visit the famous Taj Mahal. She also got a chance to see the breath-taking beauty of Kashmir and never wondered why India and Pakistan were fighting over it. Once she was invited to the home of India's minister of foreign affairs. He asked her a question: "Rebecca, what is the colour of that wall?"

Rebecca looked at the wall and replied, "It's white."

The minister said, "I see a blue wall."

Rebecca looked at the wall again, certain her eyes were not deceiving her.

"It's white, sir" she repeated.

The minister said, "Rebecca, you will never make a politician. You should have said another colour and insisted on it. Politicians tell people what they want them to believe and hammer it home!

"If you say it loud enough," he continued, "it is he who doesn't believe who will appear a fool."

Amused, Rebecca asked him, "Is that how you go up the ladder?"

His reply was, "Of course!" They both laughed.

Prime Minister Nehru had worked very hard to try to remove the caste system. He also used to visit the Delphi school and speak to the foreign students. He introduced Rebecca to his daughter, Indira Gandhi, and to his grandchildren. He took Rebecca to visit Mahatma Gandhi's grave and told her to remember one important thing: "The British ruled us for 200 years, but the reason they failed is because of our culture. They may rule you, but you must keep your culture." The Prime

Minister also told Rebecca, "When you get to the point where you have someone who is willing to die for his people, then you will be ready to govern yourselves. Remember, power is not given; it is taken."

Rebecca never forgot his words. Years later, she asked her father, "Daddy, why did you send me to India?"

His reply was, "We loved you so much, Becca, I knew you were spoilt. I wanted you to learn to be strong. I wanted you to be among people who are like us. There, the rich are very rich and the poor, very poor. I wanted you to learn to work with those who are dirt poor. Also, they are very loving people; when they love you, they really love you." Many years later, people would wonder why Rebecca could get along so well with the rich and famous, as well as the poor and invisible. India taught her that.

Chapter Five

Engagement

Rebecca thoroughly enjoyed her first year in India and did well in her examinations. Her parents had bought her a return ticket, so she flew home for a one-month holiday. She was so excited she could barely contain herself. This time, All India Airlines took her all the way to Entebbe Airport. Her parents were there to meet her and so was the handsome young doctor, Latimer, that she had kept in touch with throughout the year. Other young Ugandan men attending the nearby university in Delhi had received a cold shoulder when they approached her. She would calmly tell them about her boyfriend in Kampala. Most of them became her good friends, though, once they got over their infatuation.

Meeting Latimer after a year made her feel shy again. She remembered the letter he had written to her almost two years earlier. She remembered how her heart had skipped a beat as she shyly took the letter and didn't read it until she got home. She showed the letter to her father. Latimer was asking her to be his special friend, his girlfriend. Her father told her to take her time in replying and make sure she knew the answer in her heart before she replied. Rebecca eventually said yes, but that only God could tell where their relationship would lead. She didn't want to make a commitment she wouldn't be able to keep! That was before she went to Nairobi and started her social work studies. So many things had happened since then, but Rebecca knew that no man she had met since then could match the character of the man she had met when she was only three years old.

Latimer's sister, Yunia and her husband, Ephraim Kamanyi, were great friends of her parents. In fact, Rebecca had been a flower girl at their wedding. Latimer's brother-in-law was now a minister in the Buganda government. When her father was a teacher at King's College Budo, Rebecca's parents took in foreign students during the holidays. During term-time, they often had students over for meals prepared by her mother and long discussions chaired by her father. That's where Rebecca and Latimer met when she was still a little girl climbing trees and he was a studious teenager studying under her father. She had noticed the handsome teenager who smiled kindly at her whenever he came over or she went over to Aunt Yunia's house, but she didn't think he really noticed her. He was so much older than her, already making adult decisions about whether to become an engineer or a doctor. He had ended up choosing medicine and graduated from the Makerere (University) College as a medical officer in 1947. Rebecca had admired Latimer from afar and kept her dreams to herself until the day he gave her that letter. Now, there he was, part of the welcome party.

After they parted from Latimer, her parents drove her home. It was hard to imagine that a whole year had gone by. The old house still looked the same: the white washed walls and the ceiling made from papyrus; the front door over which the sign 'Agenda alira...' still hung – a partial quote from Psalm 126:6 *'He who continually goes forth weeping,* bearing seed for sowing, shall doubtless come again rejoicing, bringing his sheaves with him.' *(New King James Version);* the white clock with the loud tick which told the time in Luganda (a six-hour difference) hanging on one wall; the traditional drums stationed in each corner of the sitting room, and the shield of armour high up on another wall. The old house had no electricity and in the evening, with the wooden shutters closed, the only light came from the many hurricane lamps dotted around the house. Their mother would carefully wipe the glass chimney on each lamp before lighting the lamps; it was a daily ritual.

Arnold and Joe were not there when she came home as they were still studying abroad, but Rebecca could enjoy the time spent with her youngest siblings: Myers, Tempora and little sister Damallie. She was now almost two years old. Rebecca's father came around to asking her, "Becca, do you still love Latimer?" When Rebecca responded affirmatively, he said, "Well, you must introduce him to your uncles and especially your aunts. You don't want to get married to someone your family does not know." So when Latimer wasn't on duty, he took her out on dates, and she took him to visit her aunts and uncles. She was always glad that her father had given her that good piece of advice.

They got engaged during that holiday. Rebecca had never felt so sure of anything in her life before. One evening, they went out to watch a movie at the cinema. The movie was supposed to start at 6:00 p.m. but Latimer left his work at Mulago Hospital late, so they missed that showing. Then they thought they would wait for the 9:00 p.m. show. Well, you can imagine what time Rebecca got home! She said goodnight to Latimer when he dropped her off and walked up the front door stairs. Her father opened the door even before she knocked. He said, "Becca, this is the first and last time I will wake up to open the door for you. Understood?!"

She replied, "Yes, Daddy. I'm sorry." Rest assured she never came home that late again.

It felt like the holiday was over before it began. Now it was time to return to India for the second year of her two-year programme. This time, her parents got her a ticket on the *SS*

Amra, a ship sailing from Mombasa, Kenya to Bombay, India. Her father accompanied her on the train to Mombasa as he always did. He said goodbye to her at the dock and reminded her of his admonition a year earlier: endure whatever you have to, in order to reach your goal. She watched as his tall figure became smaller and smaller until finally she could not distinguish him from the surrounding throng. She didn't know if it was the pain of leaving Latimer and her family, but the trip was arduous. They were on the high seas of the Indian Ocean for ten days. It was the monsoon season and the winds kept the ship rolling from side to side. They had been advised to make sure they always had food in their stomachs, but not too much. Thank goodness she didn't have sea sickness, but it was difficult to walk around or sit down and eat your food with the ship rolling like that. It helped that she spent most of the trip knitting sweaters: one for her father, one for her mother, one for her baby sister and one for her fiancé.

The ship landed near Bombay and Rebecca disembarked. By then, she knew a little Hindi and was able to purchase a train ticket from Bombay to New Delhi. There she hired a horse-drawn rickshaw to take her to the school. She went straight to the principal's house to announce her return. Miss Moses was surprised to see her and said, "When you didn't return on the expected date, we thought you had decided to stay at home, Rebecca. Welcome back!" She *was* glad to be back and catch up with Mary and her other friends. Soon after her return, Miss Moses announced her retirement due to illness. She called Rebecca to her house and told her, "You've always been a well-behaved girl; please do not change."

Rebecca and Latimer had kept up their romance with regular letters. She was excited to receive any letter from home, but of course his held a special place in her heart and she kept every one of them. Latimer wrote to say that he had been offered a scholarship by the British government. He was to go to England to study Child Health. It was six months into the second year of her course and Rebecca had a decision to make. If she stayed in India and finished her diploma, she would then sign up for a two-year degree course in social work. It would be another two-and-half years before she would be ready to join the work force. Latimer wanted to know if she loved him enough to abandon her studies, come home and get married, so that they could travel to England together.

Rebecca sought the advice of her friends and mentors, as well as the school principal. By this time, the school was being run by Miss Perry, an American. There were two older European ladies and a gentleman who belonged to the Moral Re-Armament movement at the school. They had befriended Mary and Rebecca and regularly took them to church and brought them home for tea and Bible discussions. Rebecca told them about the decision she had to make. All three advised her to make the choice based on whatever her heart told her, whilst they prayed for her. Rebecca knew in her heart that she wanted to be Latimer's wife more than she wanted to be a social worker. It was becoming a wife and mother that she had dreamt of most as a little girl. For better or worse, the die was cast.

She wrote to her parents informing them of her decision: she wanted to return home to get married, rather than finishing her course and joining the work force. She waited nervously for their reply. That winter, the new school principal took the foreign students to the Y.W.C.A. hostel in Shimla in the mountains of North India. It was a refreshing break from the heat and bustle of New Delhi. There were very few cars and even the rickshaws were drawn by the locals. Rebecca's parents wrote back to say that since it was *her* decision to leave school, she should never look back with regret. Perhaps her father remembered how his own father had prevented him from fulfilling his dream and taking his fiancée to England with him. Later, Rebecca found out that her maternal Aunt Hannah Tezigatwa had reminded her parents of this very thing and urged them to let her follow her heart.

Rebecca went to the school principal and informed her of her decision. Then she went back to her room and packed her things. She set sail for Africa two days later. When young doctor Latimer gave her an ultimatum, Rebecca dropped her social studies course with only three months left before she would have received her diploma! She was going home to marry the first and only love of her life. She could not imagine what lay ahead in this new journey of her life.

Chapter Six

Journey Home

Rebecca had plenty of time to mull over her decision when she took the long journey home by ship across the Indian Ocean. They set sail on a Sunday evening as the sun was setting. The glow of the retreating sun was reflected in the ripples of the lapping waves. As they set off, it seemed so peaceful, but gradually the winds picked up. She loved the sound of the waves brushing the port side of the ship and the lilt of the ship as it swayed in the wind. It was not the monsoon season this time, so the winds were gentle and playful. They seemed to be beckoning her home; to what, she did not know. For now, she could enjoy the sunny days and cool nights on the ship with the other passengers. Christmas found them on board, so there was lot of partying and merriment. Rebecca joined in with all the gusto she could muster. They stopped at a port on the islands of Seychelles on the way. She and her new friends all took a tour of the island. They welcomed in the new year together. It was 1952.

When she arrived in Mombasa, the gentleman whom her father had arranged to meet her wasn't there. Rebecca was a woman alone in a foreign land! She didn't know what to do, but before long, an Indian gentleman approached her who seemed friendly and he wanted to help. When he heard her dilemma, he offered to take her to the train station. When they got to the train station, however, Rebecca didn't have enough money to take her from Mombasa to Kampala. The kind gentleman suggested that she travel third class and see how far she could get. Rebecca didn't like that idea; the people sitting in third class looked a little threatening and she didn't speak Swahili. He then suggested that he could take her to where there were some Ugandans he knew in the city.

Rebecca got back into his car and they drove to the location. She hoped that even if she didn't know the people, they would be able to communicate in the same language, and that they could take her in until she could contact her parents. They got out of the car in front of a large building. The owner and several young ladies came out to meet them. Rebecca greeted them politely but immediately knew she couldn't spend the night here; the ladies were dressed like 'malayas' with skimpy dresses and long, painted fingernails. This must be a brothel! Back inside the car, she asked the Indian gentleman to take her to a hotel where she could book a room. After that, she asked the kind gentleman if he could show her where the nearest police station or post office was. She was becoming afraid that he was being a little *too* kind.

Walking to the post office, Rebecca noticed some people driving by in a car who stared straight at her. The car stopped, doubled back and passed her again. This time they stared at her even harder. Then they stopped and asked, "Are you Mr. Kisosonkole's daughter?"

When Rebecca replied, "Yes," they broke out in excitement. It was Mr. and Mrs. Albuquerque, her father's Goan friend and his German wife, who had meant to meet her at the dock. The trip from India to Mombasa that usually took ten days had only taken eight days, so they had not been expecting Rebecca that day. By the time they learnt that the ship had arrived, it was too late. They had been searching for her all over the town. Rebecca went back to the hotel and the train station with her new friends. They picked up all her luggage and took her back to their home. She fell asleep that night feeling warm and comfortable; thanking God that she hadn't ended up in a brothel, or deserted in a foreign land.

The Albuquerques didn't know that Rebecca was going home to get married. She didn't tell them, either. They were enjoying having her around, showing her Mombasa, letting her play with the children, Claude and Claudia, and having her help them out in their shop. Finally, Rebecca's father sent a telegram asking them to please send his daughter home so that she could get married! A few days later, Rebecca took the train from Mombasa, via Nairobi to Kampala. They had just arrived in Jinja, some 50 miles from Kampala, when she saw someone she recognised standing on the platform of the train station. It was Latimer! Along with his sister and brother-in-law. They had asked her parents if they could meet her at the train station and bring her home. In his eagerness, Latimer insisted on driving to Jinja, the town before her final destination, and meeting her there. They took her home, where her family were as excited to see her as she was to see them. It was good to be home among familiar faces. After she had had a chance to freshen up, they all went to her future sister-in-law's house for tea. Her father picked up his sister, Auntie Try, along the way. She was to be Rebecca's special 'Ssenga' (paternal aunt acting as marriage counsellor before the wedding).

At the party, Rebecca's aunt told them that her oldest son, Mbaziira, was ill and in hospital. She asked Latimer if he would check on him after the tea party. Rebecca went home with her parents in the evening. They stayed up late that Sunday night talking about India, her return trip and her upcoming nuptials. They had a good laugh when Rebecca recounted her escapades in Mombasa. It was past midnight, when they heard a car pulling up outside. It sounded like Latimer's car. But why would he be coming over so late? Was he really unable to keep

Rebecca out of his sight? They opened the door to discover that he was the bearer of bad news: Rebecca's cousin who had been in hospital had just passed away. What had begun as a day of great rejoicing had turned into a night of mourning. Rebecca and her family went straight to their aunt's house, where they spent the rest of the night trying to console her. Her son was buried on the following Tuesday. Rebecca's aunt insisted that the wedding go forward as planned on Saturday, although sadly, she would not be able to attend it.

Rebecca arrived in Kampala just one week before her wedding day. Thankfully, her mother and the family had made all the necessary arrangements, including choosing a wedding gown for her. She just had to be fitted. She was too excited to pay much attention to the details, anyway. She *had* wanted her little two-and-a-half-year old sister to be a flower girl, but her parents said, "No, she's too young and will be disruptive, crying for her mother." The night before the wedding, Rebecca's father sat her down and said, "Becca, you are still our daughter. You can change your mind right now and we'll take you back and take care of you. But once you walk down that aisle and marry Latimer, you are no longer a little girl. Don't come running to us when you're upset. If you cry, you know we will want to die. Instead, lock yourself in your room, kneel down on your bedside and tell God all about it. He will give you an answer to all your problems."

Rebecca knew how much her parents loved her and didn't doubt a word he said. As a child, Rebecca had shared everything with her father, but she implicitly understood this was no longer to be the case. She said, "Daddy, I'm ready to marry Latimer."

Her father gave her one last piece of parental advice: "Whenever you get upset, stop what you are doing, count to ten slowly, take one step at a time around the room, then continue what you were doing. If you've been crying and someone asks you what is wrong, tell them you have a cold; if you can, wash some clothes or take a walk outside and pray."

At age nineteen and very much in love, Rebecca couldn't imagine ever being upset with her sweetheart. She thanked her father and took a step in her young life that January day in 1952 that she never regretted. Neither did she forget her father's advice. It served her well through the years.

The wedding was scheduled for 10 a.m. Saturday morning on the 12th day of January, 1952 at Saint Paul's Cathedral, Namirembe. The cathedral sits on one of the original seven hills upon which Kampala was built and it overlooks the centre of the city. Kabaka Edward Mutesa II had been invited, so the ceremony had to wait for his arrival. Kabaka Mutesa was a friend of Latimer's from the days when they were schoolboys at King's College Budo, and then on the athletics team at Makerere College, which later became Makerere University. As a teenager, Rebecca had had the honour of being bridesmaid to her cousin, Damali, in 1948 – when she married Kabaka Mutesa and became his Nnabagereka (queen). The Kabaka and the Nnabagereka now honoured Latimer and her with their presence at her own wedding. As with all royalty, they were late and the ceremony didn't start until 11 a.m.

Finally, the time had come for Latimer and Rebecca to exchange their marriage vows. In the Buganda culture, a bride is usually given away by her brother. Rebecca's father insisted on being the one to give her away. He said, "That's my daughter; I'm the one who knows all about her." Rebecca had a small suitcase she had kept since she was a little girl. It contained all her little secret treasures, including the letters she had received from Latimer and other suitors. Before giving her away, Rebecca's father turned to her and asked, "Did you take your little suitcase with you? All right, remember what I said last night; there is no turning back." Then he turned and placed her hand in Latimer's hand.

Chapter Seven

Early Marriage

The wedding was a grand affair. After Latimer and Rebecca had exchanged their vows and signed the registry, they marched down the aisle of Namirembe Cathedral to Mendelssohn's *'Wedding March'*. Latimer loved classical music and it became the background music of their life story. They posed outside the cathedral for group photographs and then went to Peter Nsangi's famous photography studio with the wedding party for studio pictures. Rebecca thought he spent altogether too much time on their make-up. The reception was held at the Buganda government treasurer's house; Mr. Mpagi was Latimer's cousin and spared no effort in the preparations. There was plenty of food, soft drinks and company for everyone to have a good time. Serving soft drinks at a wedding was still a novelty then; tea was the usual offering. The after-wedding party in the village had traditional Baganda drummers and dancers hired by the king himself. They kept them up all night with the music and revelry. Rebecca's only regret was that her favourite aunt could not be present at her wedding.

The next morning, she and Latimer went to church. After lunch at the Victoria Hotel in Entebbe, followed by a short afternoon siesta, they piled into Latimer's Hillman car. Saying goodbye to friends, relatives and well-wishers, they set off for their two-day honeymoon at Mr. Mpagi's home in Kyaggwe. The brevity of their honeymoon was necessitated by Latimer's posting to a hospital upcountry. What a journey! They drove all night to a town called Serere in Bukedi District where they had been posted for the next six months. They were warmly welcomed by Dr. Nfamba (the doctor they were going to replace), his wife and the hospital staff. It was the only hospital in this small town, but they were determined to show the new doctor and his bride that they could match anything the big city had to offer. They said, "Since you're still on your honeymoon, we will prepare all your meals and take care of the household chores for the first month." Rebecca looked forward to spending that time sewing warm clothes and sweaters for their upcoming trip to England.

One week into their stay in Serere, one of Rebecca's sisters-in-law, Marion, came to stay with them. She was surprised when she didn't see Rebecca going to the kitchen.

"Don't you do any cooking here?" she asked.

"Oh, the hospital staff cook for us," Rebecca answered innocently.

"What?!" her sister-in-law retorted. Apparently she wasn't amused by Rebecca's answer. "That has to stop! If need be, I will cook for you, but we mustn't have them thinking the good doctor married a child."

She promptly asked the staff to stop cooking for them. She did have a point; some of the townsfolk thought Rebecca was Latimer's sister and would ask him if she was available. *She* couldn't help it that she still looked like a teenager; she was only nineteen years old!

It was the role of motherhood that Rebecca looked forward to most. Her skills as a housewife were not stellar; spoilt as she had been by her doting parents. Sometimes she felt overwhelmed by her new responsibilities, but Latimer was always kind to his young bride. When she was cooking, he would come and sit by the kitchen (which was separate from the rest of the house) and talk to her. When she didn't want to go out to the outhouse in the dark alone, he would accompany her. When he was on call at the hospital, Rebecca was afraid to remain in the house alone. So they would spend the night sitting up in the chair in the treatment room. Eventually, they decided it made more sense if he locked her in the house and let himself in when he came back in the middle of the night. She felt like she couldn't have asked God for a more devoted husband.

Before long, her ambitious husband had whisked Rebecca away to England where he was going to pursue the advanced diploma in Child Health. The journey took several days. They travelled by plane from Entebbe to Rome and spent a night there. Then they made a second stop, she couldn't remember where, before they finally boarded a plane to England. Thankfully, they were met at the airport and taken to a hotel where they spent the first night. From there, they travelled to Wolverhampton in the Midlands, which was to be their home for next nine months.

It was the beginning of summer, so the weather was warm and pleasant. The spring rains had produced plenty of green pastures for the sheep and other cattle that dotted the English countryside. The reign of Queen Elizabeth II had just begun and the post-war recovery was in full swing. The houses in their small town were all arranged in neat little rows, the roads were all tarmacked and there was running water and electricity in every house. The neighbourhood had been integrated by the post-war influx of immigrants from several colonial countries. Everyone was so kind and welcoming. Latimer started his studies immediately, so Rebecca had plenty of time to pursue her own interests. She joined a local social worker, Lady Alma and started making rounds with her at the local hospitals. When she became pregnant, Lady Alma made sure she started antenatal care and was there for her through the remainder of her pregnancy. Rebecca never forgot Lady Alma's kindness;

she gave her three or four dozen nappies when she delivered her baby and Rebecca had enough to last through the next four babies. When Rebecca was getting close to full term and expressed her fears of the impending labour, she told her, "Remember this, Rebecca; every mother you see has been through the pain of childbirth."

Latimer could not be there for the birth of their first child in March of 1953 because it coincided with his examinations. By the time he arrived at the hospital, Rebecca had already delivered their son and written to her mother to thank her for having all of them. Her mother had gone through this eight times! She had helped her mother take care of most of her younger siblings, but Rebecca couldn't begin to describe the pain and then the joy of hearing her own baby cry for the first time; realising that she was now a mother! In those days, new mothers were kept in hospital for ten days, even after a normal delivery. The first seven days, they were not allowed to get out of bed, which would be considered bad form today. The last three days, they were finally taken to the nursery and taught how to take care of their newborn baby. By the time Rebecca was ready to leave the hospital, Latimer was in Scotland, where they spent the last three months of their stay. Rebecca remained in London for ten more days with friends, before joining him in Edinburgh.

Latimer and Rebecca named their firstborn Adam. They were so sure it was going to be a boy, they had only picked out boy's names. Not only was he their first, Adam happened to be the first name of Latimer's maternal grandfather. His middle name was to be John, after Latimer's father, Yokana Kamya. They also gave him the requisite clan name. In Buganda, every newborn child is given a clan name, usually chosen by the paternal grandparents or a paternal aunt. It does not identify him or her with just their father, as English children are, but with all of their ancestors on their father's side. Occasionally, a name can be 'borrowed' from the mother's side of the family, but this is a rare occurrence. When a Muganda introduces themselves by their clan name, you can immediately identify which clan they belong to. Everyone in your clan is a brother or a sister, an uncle, an aunt or a grandparent.

When baby Adam was six weeks old, Rebecca said to Latimer, "It looks like the weather is getting warmer. Why don't we take the baby out?" Latimer thought that was a good idea and they went out and took a studio picture to send to their families. Then they walked around the park together for a couple of hours with the baby in his perambulator. The next day, Rebecca was horrified to see a rash all over her baby's body. She showed Latimer the rash and asked him what it was. Latimer knew immediately and had to break the news to her gently: their infant son had eczema and it might take several years for him to outgrow it. He was also at risk of developing asthma later in life. Rebecca was saddened by this news and cried as any new mother would. But she knew God would give her the strength to take care of the gift He had given her. She had to be careful with anything that touched his skin: she couldn't give him regular baths, only gentle sponge baths; no more wool, only cotton. However, the time was drawing near for them to return home. Her parents were excited and couldn't wait for them to get back to Uganda.

Chapter Eight

The Golden Years

The golden post-war optimism of the 1950s was evident in British East Africa; but things are never quite as they seem on the surface. The sun was finally setting on the British Empire and all the African colonies were demanding their independence. Unlike other territories that had been named British colonies, Uganda had been named a protectorate, largely because of the government already in place in Buganda when British explorers 'discovered' it. The Kabaka not only had a functioning lukiiko (parliament) headed by the katikkiro (prime minister) and his regents, the people were governed by lower-level chiefs ranging from ssaza (county) chiefs, gombolola (sub county) chiefs, muluka (local) chiefs and village elders. The more than forty clans also had a hierarchy of elders. On discovering this system entrenched in Buganda, the British had employed many of its leaders as governors and emissaries to other regions of their protectorate, Uganda. Luganda was established as the language of communication in many of those regions, despite the presence of a language/dialect native to each people group. Resentment was growing not only towards the British, but also towards their local representatives. The resentment was not mitigated by the fact that the Baganda were somewhat averse to being absorbed into an independent Uganda.

Latimer and Rebecca returned home in 1953 to a country on the brink of turmoil. The Kabaka (King Edward Mutesa II of Buganda) was clashing with the British governor, Andrew Cohen, for advocating for separatism for his kingdom. This was against Her Majesty's wish that Uganda not be divided in its path to independence. The matter came to a head on November 30, 1953 when the Kabaka refused to change his position and was immediately deported to England. When his sister, Nnalinya Zalwango, learnt that the Kabaka had been exiled, she collapsed. The relatives who were nearby thought she had fainted from the shock of the announcement. Latimer was doctor to the Kabaka and his family. He was called to come to her side quickly; but she was already dead. She had been the wife of Rebecca's maternal uncle, Biyimbwa, and the family was once again in mourning.

During the Kabaka's two-year exile, his male subjects refused to shave and grew beards. The older women refused to wear European-style dresses and only wore 'busutis' (traditional dress) in solidarity with the Nnabagereka in her 'widowhood'. The climate of civil disobedience was palpable. Latimer had his job at Mulago Hospital, but African doctors were still second-class staff at the hospital. They had less authority and were paid less than the British nursing sisters. By the time Rebecca's second child was born, a daughter they named Damallie after her mother, they were living in a two-room house barely making ends meet. Little comfort that all the other African doctors lived in similar conditions with their families. They couldn't have made it without the help of Rebecca's parents.

The political crisis caused by the Kabaka's exile continued until 1955 when the courts decided that the British governor had not had the authority to exile the Kabaka, and he was allowed to return as a constitutional monarch. Latimer and Rebecca couldn't help but catch the excitement in the air. One week before the Kabaka's plane landed at Entebbe airport on

October 7, 1955, there were people camped out there. Rebecca and Latimer drove to Entebbe and briefly joined the convoy of cars travelling with the Kabaka from the airport to the palace in Mengo. They had to bail out early because Rebecca was still nursing her baby daughter. The jubilant crowds lining the streets from Entebbe to Kampala literally pushed the Kabaka's car all the way (twenty-two miles) so that the driver did not have to start the engine. They were drumming and dancing and shouting, "Teyalina! Teyalina! Teyalina buyinza!" which means, "He (the governor) didn't have the authority!"

The governor's response was incredulous: "The Baganda baffle me! I thought the Baganda had become disenchanted with their Kabaka over some of his recent behaviour. I didn't realise that even if they were upset at Mutesa, they would never turn against their Kabaka!"

Life seemed to return to normal when the king was allowed to return. Latimer had been promoted to District Medical Officer and posted upcountry to Mubende – the first Ugandan to be named a district medical officer. They were treated with love and respect by the community and given a big house and servants. They would often look back and laugh, remembering the two-room house with no ceiling which they had brought their baby daughter home to. They nicknamed her 'Little Miss Active': she never would sit still. Two more daughters were born to them during this seemingly blissful period, Louise and Philippa. Louise was named after Latimer's mother, and Philippa was named for the son of their good friends in England who took care of Rebecca right after Adam was born. Each time she was getting ready to deliver, Rebecca would travel home from Mubende to her parent's house at Mulawa so that she could deliver at Old Mulago Hospital. Rebecca's little sister, Damallie, was only three years older than her firstborn. She became a part of the family and was like another daughter, but would become so much more as the years went by.

Rebecca had been vaguely aware that the Kabaka was enamoured with both her cousins, Damali and Sarah, and wasn't surprised when her cousin Sarah gave birth to Prince Ronald Muwenda Mutebi while his father was still in exile. (The story went around that the Kabaka had always been in love with Sarah, but had married Damali because she was the older sister, but Rebecca knew better). Kabaka Mutesa had a very good friend, the 'Omukama' (King) of Toro. The Kabaka would often stop by Rebecca and Latimer's home in Mubende on his way to Fort Portal in Toro. That would be a time for everyone to drop everything (except hospital staff, of course) and hold a feast in celebration of their king. One night, Rebecca thought she heard his convoy arriving in their compound. She looked out of the window and confirmed that it was indeed the Kabaka.

Latimer asked her, "Do we have any alcohol in the house?"

Rebecca replied, "No, we don't; what should we do?"

"Go and talk to him while I take the car and go and buy some alcohol from the Indian store down the street. I know they'll open for me," Latimer responded.

While Latimer quickly exited through the back door, Rebecca welcomed the guests. To buy time, she went into the kitchen and brought the Kabaka some water in a jug and a glass on a tray.

She said, "Ssebo, Omwami asoka 'kunywa olwendo lw'amazzi," meaning, "a gentleman must always drink some water first."

He looked at her with surprise and said, "How do you know that saying?"

Rebecca replied, "Ssebo, ndi mukyala Muganda" which means, "Sir, I am a Muganda woman."

While they were still chatting, Latimer returned with the alcohol. The Kabaka and Latimer stayed up talking and laughing all night long.

On another occasion, the Kabaka noticed an area rug they had and commented on how nice it was. Latimer said, "Sir, would you like me to roll it up so that you can take it with you?"

He replied, "Eh, if I like something everywhere I go, do I get to take it?"

"Well, if you like it..." was Latimer's response.

The Kabaka then asked, "So, if I say I like Rebecca, do I get to take her?"

Latimer didn't hesitate. "No, that would involve a fight." They all laughed.

It was the comfortable jesting of friends who had known each other since their carefree high school days. However, the Kabaka's entourage did indeed regularly gather up any utensils he had been served in as rightly belonging to him. It was universally understood that if the Kabaka looked at anything in his kingdom with a favourable eye, whether a wagon or a woman, it was his for the taking. Conversely, when the Omukama of Toro visited and they tried to give him or his entourage any gifts, he always refused on behalf of his entourage. His reply was, "If we keep taking things whenever we visit, what will you have left?"

Latimer and Rebecca were living in what later became known as 'the Lost Counties' of Mubende district. These counties had been annexed by Buganda from the neighbouring Kingdom of Bunyoro during the turbulent years of British colonialism in the late 1800s. In an effort to impress the people of these counties and prevent them from passing a referendum that would return them to Bunyoro, the Buganda government was spending lots of money building houses and schools and planting orchards in Mubende district. Rebecca had become a close friend of Mrs. Bazley, the District Commissioner's wife and together they held seminars for the women; teaching them to read, sew and take better care of their children.

In addition to holding clinics in various locations around the region, Latimer built a house next to the main hospital where family members of those hospitalised could reside. Rebecca and Latimer owned two lorries that they sent around to the villages collecting food, clothes and household goods to be sold at a market that was held weekly within the town. All the proceeds from the market were being used to build a church in the town centre. By the time Latimer and Rebecca left Mubende, the church had almost been completed. Latimer's dedication to his work as the District Medical Officer in Mubende was awarded with a 'Member of the British Empire' (M.B.E.) medal for meritorious service from the Queen of England.

Chapter Nine

Motherhood

They left Mubende in 1959. The people they had worked with and cared for for four years were sad to see them go. They threw a big farewell party for them and gave them numerous gifts. They returned to Kampala to prepare for their next trip to England, and Latimer briefly returned to his job at Mulago Hospital. Their second son, Wilfred, was born during this time. They named him after their good friend, Wilfred Sheldon, who had been instrumental in helping them go to England the first time. Latimer had been awarded another scholarship, this time by the Buganda government, and was heading back to England to study for his membership in the Royal College of Physicians (M.R.C.P.). He had been granted a sabbatical for this. It was baffling, but the government would only pay for them to take two of their five children with them. Rebecca and Latimer sat down to discuss their options.

Rebecca considered staying in Uganda with the children and letting Latimer go alone. Everyone said, 'no'. Should they take the two youngest children who still needed their mother so much? Or should they take the two eldest who would benefit most from going to school in England? They chose the latter option, believing that what would benefit the older children, would eventually be passed on to the younger. They would divide the youngest three children between her parents and Latimer's sister, Yunia. She had a daughter, Susan, about the same age as one of their own. Daudi, the manservant who had taken care of Rebecca and her brothers since Dolphe was a baby, was still in her parents' service. He told Rebecca to go to England with her husband; he and a new nanny would help her mother take care of any children she had to leave behind. Sadly, Daudi passed away while Rebecca was still in England. Upon learning of his death, his relatives had come and taken his body away for burial. On her return, Rebecca tried in vain to discover where he had been buried. She was eternally grateful for his service to her mother and herself, but he had no children upon whom she could bestow her gratitude.

It was during this interim period of waiting to go to England that an incident occurred that reminded Rebecca of her growing responsibilities. Her mother was now a successful businesswoman, living and working in Mbale, over 130 miles east of Kampala. She managed a fleet of buses which plied the Kampala - Mbale route. Her father was working for the Buganda government as a school superintendent, inspecting their schools. Rebecca asked Latimer if, before they left for England, she could go and visit her mother in Mbale. Latimer agreed and Rebecca decided to take the two youngest children with her for a week or two's holiday. Her father drove them up to Mbale one Friday. Her mother was overjoyed to see them, especially her two youngest grandchildren. She fussed over them and showed them off to all her friends and neighbours.

The next day, they were sitting down to supper when, who should show up? Latimer had driven up to Mbale with the other three children. The children were happy to have the family all together again, but Latimer had come to report that he could not take care of the three older children alone. They needed their mother; to feed them, bathe them and put them to bed. Either his wife could come home with him, or he would leave the older children there. Rebecca's mother protested that the visit had been too short, but Rebecca made up her mind quickly that it was best for the children if they all went home. They had enrolled the older children in a Moslem school in Kampala where they were learning English in preparation for their trip. She couldn't afford to have them miss out on that.

As she watched her children grow up, Rebecca always wondered whether they had made the right decision. There were very few times she saw Latimer cry during their twenty-seven-year marriage. One was when their second daughter, Louise, arrived in England thin and scraggly, after only a few months of living with her aunt. She had caught the measles and whooping cough. They had only learnt after their arrival that the government would have paid for *three* children to accompany them to England. So they arranged for the wife of a colleague, Dr. Joseph Lutwama, to bring their second daughter to England. Luckily, she was a clever little girl and caught up with her age mates at the nursery school quickly. One day she came home and told her mother, "Mummy, I don't want to go to that baby school anymore. I want to go to the big school with Adam and Damallie."

Living in Hampstead, England in 1960 with three or four children under age 10 was quite different from when they had come over as a newly-wed couple in 1952. Latimer was working at the Hospital for Sick Children at Great Ormond Street. With only Latimer's stipend to support them, times were hard, but Rebecca was up to the challenge. They were renting a house at 8, Well Walk in Hampstead from Dr. and Mrs. Welbourne, who were working in Uganda at the time. Latimer and Rebecca's family occupied two floors that had the living room, dining room, kitchen and bathroom on the main level and the bedrooms on the first floor. Throughout their residence, they had other family members or friends living in the loft on the second floor. Rebecca scrubbed those staircases every week throughout their tenure, even during her pregnancy, and swore to herself she would never again live in a storeyed house. She had never shunned hard work and did whatever it took to keep her home clean, do the laundry, provide healthy meals and keep the children out of Latimer's way so that he could study. Hampstead heath was not far from the house and she would take the children out to play on the heath. She herself took a course in Childcare and First Aid.

Rebecca got the mumps for the first time while she was in England. She had never had the mumps as a child because her mother didn't allow anyone who was ill, child or adult, anywhere near her children. Rebecca learnt to delegate responsibilities. Her brother, Arnold, was living with them while he attended Dental School. He would take the children to school on the train in the morning and Rebecca would pick them up in the afternoon. Later, her brothers Joe and Myers came to study in England as well; Joe was taking a course in Radio and TV broadcasting and Myers, a course in Agriculture. Firstborn Adam became adept at making the tea and setting the table. Eldest daughter Damallie helped with the baby. The other children helped with washing up the dishes after meals and even Latimer helped after supper. Television had become a staple in English homes by then and that's when Latimer and Rebecca decided that, when they returned to Uganda, they would *not* have a television in the house. They saw how all-absorbing it was to their little children's minds and kept their promise not to have a television until the youngest were teenagers.

The children were attending All Souls School. One day, Rebecca thought to herself: 'With eight-year old Adam in charge, they can probably start travelling home on the train by themselves.' The first time she experimented with letting them travel alone, she quickly skipped off the train after they had all boarded. She hoped the children would proceed on their journey without incident and get off the train when they reached Hampstead. Wishful thinking! Adam screamed at the top of his lungs until the conductor stopped the train and Rebecca was allowed to re-board. So the next time, she simply told them that she would not be there to pick them up. Somehow, they made it home alone and thereafter, it became the routine. It wasn't without incident, though.

One day, the children were playing on the train and missed their stop. Hampstead was the last underground stop; but suddenly the train was flooded with broad daylight. So with tickets in hand, they had to make their way back to Hampstead. They were so proud of themselves when they made it! On another occasion, they were at the station waiting for the train when Damallie remembered she had left her homework at school. Adam grabbed his two sisters and they headed out of the station. Rush hour always filled the streets and stations with crowds of people of all ages moving in every possible direction. They ran back to the school and had managed to make their way back to the station when Adam and Damallie realised that Louise was no longer with them. Fear gripped their little hearts. How were they going to explain to their mother that they had lost their little sister? They headed down the stairs to the interior of the station. They were standing on the platform, wondering what to do next, when an Englishwoman came walking towards them holding Louise by the hand. Compared to the way *they* were feeling, Louise didn't look perturbed at all. Adam grabbed both his sisters by the hand now and proceeded quickly onto the train. They were late for his favourite TV programme!

The next time Rebecca saw tears in Latimer's eyes was when they decided to send their new baby daughter, Elizabeth, home to Rebecca's mother. She was sent home to be company for her brother so that older sister, Philippa, could come to England. Philippa arrived plump and healthy, so Rebecca was sure the baby would also be lovingly cared for by her mother. When Philippa arrived, she declared to her mother, "That little baby you sent to grandma cries all the time. Grandma is the only one who can keep her quiet!" Although they had sent the baby home so that Wilfred could have a playmate, Philippa was quite certain she wouldn't fill the role. The baby wasn't old enough yet to play with Wilfred in the sand!

At the first sign of snow, Philippa ran outside bare-footed to play in the lovely 'white sand'.

The others came in shouting, "Mummy, mummy, your daughter is playing in the snow without shoes or a hat!"

She didn't like the cold and the next time Uncle Myers came to visit, Philippa said, "Uncle, go and get Jjajja's car so that we can go home."

Although they sent their infant daughter home on the plane accompanied by close family friends, it felt like they were sending an impersonal post-paid parcel. At the airport, Rebecca placed her infant daughter in her friend's arms, complete with a small suitcase of her clothes. The baby reached back for her and immediately started crying. It was all that Rebecca could do not to grab her and take her back. She rode back from the airport with Latimer and the other children, tears still rolling down her face. She couldn't help but remember the time she had left baby Elizabeth in the house alone. She had run down to the laundrette for just a few minutes, but by the time she returned, the baby had crawled out of her playpen. Her dress was caught on one of the stakes and she was half dangling out of it. That's when Rebecca had decided she needed her mother's help.

The day after they handed over the baby, they rang her parents in Kampala expecting to hear that the baby had been safely delivered to them; only to discover that baby Elizabeth had not arrived yet. A phone call from their friends at the airport confirmed the report: their flight had been cancelled due to wind and fog and they had to spend the night at a nearby hotel. They had been assigned a new flight and they were just about to board.

SEMEI KIYIMBA *   HAM MUKASA *   BULASIO MWEBE *   * TEFIRO KISOSONKOLE
SIR DAUDI CHWA *

Kabaka Daudi Chwa II and his guardian Tefiro Kisosonkole (right).

Kupliano (2nd left) and his siblings Try,
Marjorie and Christopher, circa 1912.

Rebecca (centre) and her brothers Arnold, Joe
and Dolphe with a friend, circa 1942.

Rebecca (back row, centre) with her parents and siblings. 1950

Rebecca as a student in India. 1951

Kabaka Edward Mutesa II and Damali Kisosonkole's wedding. 1948 (Rebecca is 2nd left)

Latimer and Rebecca's wedding. Kabaka and Nnabagereka seated on left. Namirembe Cathedral. 1952

Latimer and Rebecca with their firstborn, Adam. 1953

Rebecca with children Adam, Damallie and Louise. 1961

Rebecca's children Philippa and Wilfred. 1961

Rebecca with children Damallie, Louise,
Elizabeth and Adam. 1961

Latimer and Rebecca with Philippa, Adam,
Louise, Damallie and Uncle Myers. 1962

Rebecca with her sister and the children
at Nakasero, circa 1965.

Chapter Ten

Independence

Latimer was awarded his membership in the Royal College of Physicians in April and they returned to Uganda in July of 1962. He was the first Ugandan to be awarded his M.R.C.P. in Paediatrics. Adam was excited because he was going to see his little brother for the first time in two years. He went on a shopping spree with his mother and insisted that they buy his brother every kind of toy imaginable. Much to his dismay, three-year old Wilfred was not as appreciative as he had hoped. He proceeded to dismantle or destroy every toy his brother had carefully selected for him. Wilfred and Elizabeth, nicknamed Bessie, were indeed well cared for by their grandparents and the nanny Lebeka, but neither one recognised their parents when the family returned. The children who had gone to England with them came home speaking very little Luganda, even though they could still understand it. They decided to get the children registered in an English-speaking primary school.

Latimer and Rebecca's second homecoming was as exciting as the first. The country was abuzz with the anticipation of impending independence from the British colonial government. They had missed the first elections in which Benedicto Kiwanuka had been elected Prime Minister. The second election's outcome seemed to run straight down tribal and religious lines, with the Catholics voting for the Democratic Party (DP) and the Protestants of the Uganda People's Congress (UPC) and Kabaka Yekka (KY) – 'Only the King' uniting to defeat the Democratic Party. It introduced them to a name that would come to signify the death of everything they held sacred: Apollo Milton Obote, a politician from the northern tribe of Lango and leader of the Uganda People's Congress.

The country was going to be a republic with both a president and a prime minister, with the real power being held by the Prime Minister, Milton Obote. Kabaka Sir Edward Mutesa II was offered the Presidency of Uganda. He accepted. Latimer saw this as a bad move and said to his friend, "Why would you, a king by birthright, stoop to a position such as president that requires election and appointment?" His warning fell on deaf ears; the Kabaka considered the move politically expedient to hold together the coalition of the two parties that had won the election. There was an air of optimism: the Africans would take over their country and work together to govern and build an even better 'Pearl of Africa'.

When Rebecca and Latimer first got married, her father had bequeathed a beautiful parcel of land to her. The land was at Kyaliwajjala, about ten miles from the city centre. They had built a small house on the property which they occupied briefly before their second trip to England. They hoped one day to build a farm there, on which they could live when Latimer retired. Rebecca still owned the two lorries her father had given her as well, one a Leyland, the other an Albion. They were doing good business with them and eventually built two rental houses with the profits; but it was the house on the farm that was their real dream. They imagined living there as they grew old and grey together, surrounded by their orchards and livestock; welcoming their grandchildren and teaching them how to live off the land.

On their return to Uganda, Latimer took a job as a senior consultant to the government in the department of Paediatrics at Mulago Hospital, in Kampala. At first, they went back to living in their own house outside the city and Rebecca tried her hand at cultivating a vegetable garden. Rebecca junior (Becky) was born the following year. The day of her birth, Rebecca placed a small suitcase in the boot of Latimer's car. After dropping the children off at school, she asked him to drop her off at his sister Yunia's house. When he came to pick her up in the evening, Rebecca asked to be taken to Mulago Hospital because her labour pains were getting closer. They rushed to hospital with all the children in the car. Latimer knew his way around the hospital and they quickly commandeered a stretcher to rush her to the maternity ward. But Becky couldn't wait. She was born just inside the maternity ward, on the stretcher. A short while later, the children waiting in the car were excited to see their father standing in the hospital window, waving to them and showing them their new baby sister. They were so surprised to see the squirming, light-skinned little baby; it had all happened so fast. With the knowledge that their mother was fine, too, the children chattered excitedly all the way home.

Rebecca wanted to teach her growing brood some important lessons. One of them was never to tell a lie. She told them this story, which they often asked her to repeat:

> *"Once upon a time, there was a little girl called Jessica who lived with her Mummy and Daddy. Her Daddy was away at work all day because he was a doctor. She had a nanny to take care of her at home because her Mummy was ill and had to take special medicine for her illness. Jessica was curious about what was inside the medicine cabinet above the bathroom sink, but she was too short to reach the cabinet door and no one would lift her up to see. One day, Jessica pulled a chair into the bathroom, climbed up onto the sink and opened the medicine cabinet. What a treasure to feast her eyes on! There*

were several bottles of different sizes and colours, most filled with little round tablets. Jessica reached out to move a brown bottle aside so that she could see the green one behind it. The next thing she knew, there was a crash and the brown bottle had bounced off the sink and splintered on the floor. All the little white tablets that had been inside were scattered all over the bathroom floor too.

Jessica jumped down from her perch onto the floor and was getting ready to run away, when she paused. Daddy had taken Mummy to see the doctor. The only other person in the house was the nanny, and the last time she had seen her she was outside hanging up clothes on the clothes line. Jessica couldn't hear anyone moving around in the house and she peeped out of the window. Her nanny was still outside. Jessica ran to the kitchen and grabbed the broom and dustpan to sweep up all the broken glass. But first, she picked up every little white tablet that she could find on the bathroom floor. She found another brown medicine bottle in the cabinet that was only half full and put the rest of the tablets into it. By the time her nanny came back into the house, she had not only cleaned up and disposed of all the evidence, she was back in her bedroom calmly playing with her baby dolls.

A week later, Jessica's mother took a turn for the worse. She was rushed to hospital but only lived a few more days. Jessica was very sad when her mother passed away, but at least she still had her Daddy and her nanny. Several months passed and Jessica was seeing less and less of her Daddy. She thought he must be working very hard at the hospital. One day, she was sitting in the bathtub and her nanny was kneeling beside it when she started crying.

Jessica asked her, 'Nanny, why are you crying?'

At first her nanny just kept on crying but finally she told Jessica, 'Because today your Daddy is going to be punished for killing your Mummy.'

Jessica was shocked. She asked her, 'Why do they think Daddy killed Mummy?'

Her nanny replied, 'The police found a medicine bottle in which her tablets had been mixed. She died because she was taking too much medicine. Because your Daddy is a doctor, the judge thinks he's the only one who could have known which two medicines to mix so that your Mummy died.'

Jessica looked at her nanny in disbelief. 'Daddy is not the one who mixed the tablets. I dropped one of Mummy's medicine bottles by mistake one day. I swept up the tablets and put them into another brown bottle. Then I swept up all the glass.'

Jessica's nanny jumped up from the floor. 'Did you really do it, Jessica?'

When Jessica said 'Yes,' her nanny ran down the stairs and out of the house as fast as she could. She ran down the street, turned the corner and raced down to the courthouse as fast her legs could carry her. She could barely speak when she got there but, between breaths, she asked the judge where Jessica's father was. She told him that she knew the truth about what had happened; that he was not guilty of killing his wife.

He answered her, 'Ma'am, you're too late! Doctor Smith was executed this morning.'

So Jessica lost her Mummy and her Daddy because she did not tell the truth!" The moral of the story is that you must always own up to the truth, no matter how scared you might be of the consequences.

Chapter Eleven

Growing Family

With the help of Ephraim, Latimer's brother-in-law, the children started attending Nakasero Primary School; a school that had once been exclusively for European children. Following English tradition, each child was registered at the school by their 'Christian' name followed by their father's surname, rather than their clan name. For example, Adam was registered as Adam Musoke instead of Adam Kabali. Rebecca remembered with irony the time when her father had taken her to the same European Primary School as a little girl to watch a play. She was so excited and couldn't wait to get inside. However, to her disappointment and that of her father, they were turned away because they were African. They had only been allowed to stand in the window and watch the play from there. As fate would have it, Rebecca's daughter, Damallie, was chosen out of the whole school to present a bouquet of flowers to the Duchess of Kent when she represented the Queen of England at Uganda's independence in October of 1962.

It was not practical for the children to come home for lunch during the day. They would walk to the YWCA (Young Women's Christian Association) canteen and then back to school. Latimer would pick them up after completing his hospital rounds at the end of the day. This proved to be very tiring for the children.

So they bought a second car, a DKW. Rebecca's father patiently taught her to drive in her little car. One day, her father took her eldest son, Adam, to visit a neighbouring county. When it got dark, they realised their lights were out and decided to spend the night there. Well, there were no telephones in the village in those days, so Rebecca's mother was worried sick about them. The next morning, they were driving home at breakneck speed when they met Rebecca and her mother coming to their rescue in the little DKW! Rebecca knew she was ready to start driving herself around. She started taking a picnic lunch for the children. She would pick them up and drive to a quiet location for them to eat their picnic lunch. Sometimes, the milk had already gone sour in the hot sun and the children couldn't drink it; but they were simply happy that they didn't have to go to the YWCA anymore. At the end of the day, Rebecca could pick them up at a more reasonable hour than their father had.

Eventually, Rebecca convinced Latimer that they should move into government housing so that the children could be nearer their school and participate in extracurricular activities. They looked at a number of houses on Nakasero Hill and finally chose 12, Nakasero Road. The house on Nakasero Road had a front porch, a large living/dining room area, a kitchen, three bedrooms and a bathroom all on one level! It became their home for the next four years. The primary school was close enough that the children could walk to and from school, except when it rained. In those instances, Latimer would drive them to school in his Mercedes-Benz on the way to work. If they were not ready in time, he would leave without them and Rebecca would somehow pile them all into her little DKW. The children could now participate in after-school activities such as choir practice and sports programmes. Another advantage was that the children were able to start attending the Crusaders Programme, a Sunday School programme administered by the nearby All Saints Church. Rebecca believed that the programme would lay a good Christian foundation for her children. She firmly believed in the scripture, 'Train up a child in the way he should go and when he is old he will not depart from it'. Proverbs 22:6.

Rebecca stayed at home to take care of their expanding family, which now included Latimer's four older children, Henry, Patrick, Eva and Harriet. They had been cared for by their Aunt Marion while Rebecca and Latimer were away in England. After some soul-searching, and despite criticism from her extended family, Rebecca accepted Latimer's other children into her home and did her best to treat them like her own. They were all in boarding school but would come home during the holidays. Both Latimer and Rebecca felt it was important that the young teenagers receive their father's hands-on guidance. Latimer wanted to instil his sense of independence in all his children. He liked to say, "Everyone sits on their own bottom."

With eleven children in the house during the holidays, there was a lot of cooking, cleaning, washing, ironing and shopping to do. However, unlike her stint in London, Rebecca had plenty of help: a nanny to help with the children, a cook who also helped with household chores and another to keep up the compound. The advantage of having a large family was that the older children could help take care of the little ones, and they never lacked for playmates.

Rebecca was there when the children came home for lunch and would have tea ready for them when they came home from school in the afternoon. She would help them with their homework, especially reading and multiplication tables. She had to keep a special eye out for Adam who liked to sneak in, drop off his school bag in his room and then dash off to play with his friend, Jimmy, before doing his homework. Rebecca never insisted that her children take afternoon naps. She had hated the ritual during her own childhood and promised herself that her children would have free reign to play every afternoon. However, Rebecca soon realised that she needed an afternoon nap herself, so she would lie down on one of their beds and let them play around her. She got more rest this way than if she tried to rest in her own room.

Rebecca's sister, Damallie, was now in high school and living with them during term time. She was the perfect mother's helper, but young enough to join in all the children's activities. They played a lot of indoor games but spent much of their playtime outdoors. Despite their mother's handicap, they all learnt to ride a bicycle. They took turns riding their one bicycle up and down the driveway until Adam (or Wilfred) crashed it into the garage. The children loved to stand on the front porch and sing for the passers-by, who were usually an indifferent audience. Their favourite song was '*Got no silver, got no gold; what we've got will serve us all; we've got the sun in the morning and the moon at night!*'

Baby Becky didn't like being left at home alone when her siblings went to school. She was adventurous and always wanting to try new things. Once she tried to pull herself up on the bumper of Mummy's car just as her mother pulled away. She was only bruised a little bit. On another occasion, her older siblings were pushing her down the hill on her tricycle when it tipped over and sent her head first into the ground. That time, she had to be rushed to hospital for a few stitches. A couple of times she locked herself in the bathroom and had to be coaxed out by Auntie Damallie, who instructed her to drop the key on the floor so that her aunt could reach it. Maybe she didn't want everyone getting into her business anymore.

One day, Rebecca and Damallie couldn't find Baby Becky. She was now a toddler; so after looking all over the house, they started searching the neighbourhood. Eventually, they found her at the little nursery school across the street. At two-and-a-half years old she had made up her own mind when she would start school. It was scary to think how she had managed to cross the street! They had once rushed to that very intersection one evening after hearing the noise of metal scraping metal.

Latimer was not home yet and they thought he might have been involved in the accident. Thankfully, it wasn't him, but he pulled up just as they got to the accident scene. He wasn't amused to find Rebecca and Damallie standing there. "Who is taking care of my children while you are out here gawking at the accident?" he barked.

Being a doctor, Latimer didn't believe in over-medicating the children. The only medicines he allowed in the house were those for asthma and malaria. If a child was coughing but did not have a fever, he would say, "Give the child some sweet water to drink." One day, after treating daughter Louise with an inhaler for an asthma attack, Rebecca set off with her to hospital. The inhaler did not appear to be ameliorating her symptoms and she could not convince Latimer to take the symptoms seriously. After Rebecca drove off with their daughter, though, he jumped into his car and followed them. Rebecca thought to herself, 'He might be the doctor, but I know my children better.'

Latimer was a loving but strict disciplinarian with the children, much like her own father had been. His bark was far worse than his bite, though, and the children were more afraid of the sound of his temper than any spanking. Whatever Rebecca thought about his strict discipline, she realised what a positive effect it was having on her children's drive to succeed. They coveted his approval and wouldn't dream of being truant from school. She was always there to soften the landing at the end of term, whether their report cards were glowing or grim.

It seemed like every year someone had major examinations to sit for: Primary leaving, Ordinary-level or Advanced-level. Sometimes they had one at each examination level in the same year. In the early days, Rebecca had worried that some of her children might fail like she had; but eventually, she stopped worrying and left them in God's hands. Their eldest moved on from Nakasero to Makerere College School and the girls went on to Gayaza High School year by year. Louise went on government scholarship because she had come in second in the country in her primary leaving examinations. Their second son went on to King's College Budo, his parent's alma mater.

Latimer insisted that Rebecca visit the girls regularly in boarding school. Remembering her own experience in boarding school, Rebecca took that task to heart, visiting them at least twice every month. She would take a few extra shillings for Philippa so that she could buy herself the kabalagala (pancakes) she loved. Whatever else Latimer and Rebecca couldn't give them, loving support and a good education would not be one of them. She was happy with every one of their scholastic achievements, big or small. It wasn't true that mothers only cared about good manners and fathers, only the children's grades. Latimer cared just as much about the children's manners and wouldn't tolerate a report card that said 'bad manners' or 'laziness'. Rebecca had given up her career for Latimer and the children; they never gave her any reason to regret her decision.

One day, the whole family returned home from a visit to Latimer's aunt with a live goat in tow. The gift had been trussed up and placed in the boot of the car with its legs securely fastened together. Latimer drew up in front of their house at Nakasero and instructed the boys to open the boot and secure the goat to a nearby tree. Somehow, the goat had worked itself free; as soon as the boot was opened, it scrambled out and took off up the driveway. Latimer growled at the boys and told them to go after it. They were not to return without it. Adam, Henry and Patrick combed the whole neighbourhood until it was too dark to see into the shadows. They went up to the Uganda Television headquarters and asked the askari (security guard) if he had seen a 'ngombe' running by. The problem was, they were trying to convey their question in broken Swahili and were actually asking him whether he had seen a cow. He kept asking them whether they were really looking for a 'ngombe' in the middle of the city, and they kept on answering 'yes'. They came home 'sans goat' with their 'tails between their legs'. Some other family must have enjoyed a hearty meal that Christmas.

Chapter Twelve

Politics

As the Indian foreign minister had predicted, Rebecca paid little attention to politics except as it affected her own family. But she could not keep her blinders on for long. Soon there were rumblings of discord between the backers of the Prime Minister, Dr. Milton Obote, and the Baganda; who accepted no higher authority on earth than that of their Kabaka. In February 1966, Dr. Obote abrogated the constitution of 1962 (created at the time of independence) and declared himself the executive president. The Kabaka was no longer the president of Uganda! In response, the Buganda government demanded that Dr. Obote's government leave the capital city of Kampala, which is located in the centre of Buganda.[2] As close as her family was to the royal family, Rebecca could not but be aware that when the battle came to a head, it would hit close to home.

In March of that year, there was a major earthquake along the fault line in the rift valley near the Ruwenzori Mountains. The epicentre of the 6.8 magnitude earthquake was located along the Uganda/Congo border, but its effects could be felt throughout the region of East and Central Africa. Buildings were damaged and there was loss of life on both sides of the border. To Ugandans, it was representative of the battle going on for control of the nation. The battle *did* eventually come to a

- 75 -

head. On May 24, 1966, the army stormed the Kabaka's palace in Mengo at the command of Dr. Milton Obote. They were led by General Idi Amin. He and the president were both from the north of Uganda. Kabaka Edward Mutesa tried to defend his palace. His subjects had mounted barricades at the gates using old vehicles and furniture and dug trenches to protect the main gate. World War II veterans known as Kawonawo (survivors) loyal to the king were stationed inside and outside the main gate. After eight hours of assault, with the odds heavily stacked against them, the Kabaka and a few of his men scaled the palace wall to escape the escalating conflict.

The people of Kampala heard gun and mortar fire throughout the day and night despite the rain. In the morning, they could see smoke spiralling from the palace. Latimer and Rebecca knew that it was the end of life as they had known it. They were concerned about the safety of family members who lived or worked in the palace and later learnt that one of Latimer's brothers, Masembe, had been killed. They heard rumours that the Kabaka may have escaped, but it was still uncertain. The next day, Latimer went to work as he usually did at Mulago Hospital and Rebecca took the children to school to keep a semblance of normalcy. Rebecca was alone with the help at home when a gentleman she had previously known only as an acquaintance came to the door. She cautiously let him in, uncertain if he was bringing good or bad news. The gentleman made a request of her that Rebecca knew would require her to make a possibly fateful decision.

The gentleman appeared to want privacy and Rebecca took him to a private area of the house. What he told her sent chills down her spine: Yes, the Kabaka had escaped from the palace; he was safe at an undisclosed location, but he needed a car to get him out of the city and to the border so that he could leave the country. They had managed to locate a car in a showroom that couldn't be tracked, but the owner wanted collateral in case the car wasn't returned. With her heart pounding in her throat, Rebecca didn't hesitate. She knew exactly what she had to do. Saying a quick prayer under her breath, she went to her bedroom and found the log book of Latimer's Mercedes-Benz. She gave the log book to the gentleman to hand over to the owner of the showroom until the getaway car would be returned.

It wasn't until days later that they all learnt that, although he was slightly injured during the escape, the Kabaka had made it safely into exile in England. Latimer's log book was returned and only then did his wife have the courage to tell him what she had done. If she had had to, Rebecca would have been willing to give the very title of the land they hoped to one day build the farm on. The Kabaka had escaped from the palace basically unharmed, but many of the faithful Kawonawo had paid for it with their lives. The political fallout continued. Latimer's closest brother, Cranimer Kabali, was jailed and then released. Their brother-in-law, Ephraim Kamanyi, who had been a minister in the now defunct Buganda government, no longer had a job when he returned from an assignment in America. Latimer and Rebecca let his family move into their house near Kyaliwajjala and start a farm of their own. Early the following year, there was an attempt on the life of the president which mistakenly hit the vice president's car. Ephraim's son, Dan, was implicated in the plot. A year later, Ephraim and his son, Dan, were tried, convicted and imprisoned for 'acts of treason against the state'.[3]

The day that Ephraim was detained, Latimer and Rebecca had passed by their home with the children after visiting her parents at Mulawa. It was drizzling as they drove up to the farm house. Ephraim came out and said, "Oh, it's you" as though he was expecting someone else. He was generally a quiet man, but that evening he was particularly subdued as he spoke to Latimer. Rebecca and the children did not get out of the car because of the rain, and after chatting for a short while, they drove off. She remembered looking back and seeing him standing in the rain.

He cut a lonely figure in the growing darkness. The next day, they received the news that he had been detained. Rebecca's favourite sister-in-law, Yunia, disappeared.

Rebecca and Latimer were questioned by the authorities after the arrest of her in-laws, because they had been living on their land at the time when illegal guns were found in their possession. She had suspected that her in-laws might still be involved in politics after the coup, but since her husband feigned ignorance, Rebecca remained mum on the subject. Latimer did not maintain contact with his sister after her disappearance, but sent a message through one of his friends – advising her to shave her head, so that when her hair grew back, it would be white. He also sent her the medicine she needed to control her blood pressure and told her to add bitter tomatoes to her diet. Yunia remained in hiding for almost two years. When she finally came out of hiding, she gave herself up, saying, "I got tired of the isolation." She, too, was imprisoned for several months as an accomplice to her husband and son. Rebecca and Latimer did their best to support the rest of the children, especially their youngest, Susan.

Times were changing, but Rebecca was going to make sure the children were safe and protected from the turmoil all around. Thankfully, her parents were alive and well and there to give her the support she needed. Three of her brothers got married: Arnold, Joe and Dolphe, and little sister Damallie left for further studies in England. Latimer's eldest son, Henry, had already left for further studies in America. In 1967, they moved again when Latimer was appointed to the medical faculty at Makerere University. The university campus was a closed community and Rebecca immediately felt safer there with the children. They had to decline the first house they were offered. It only had three bedrooms; too small for their growing family. The house at 56, University Road was bigger than the one they had moved out of, with a screened in porch, four bedrooms and eventually, a second bathroom. Even more importantly, it had a large compound in which the children could play. There were numerous trees for them to climb, and on one side of the house, a rose garden where you could retreat to meditate. It was no longer a short walk to school, so Latimer had to drive the children to school in the morning, bring them home at lunchtime and take them back in the afternoon. They walked the two miles home at the end of the school day.

It was also in 1967 that Latimer and Rebecca decided to go ahead with their plans to start a farm. This meant taking out a sizeable loan; which could take years to pay off. Rebecca had tried her hand at raising egg layer chickens in Mubende and hadn't had much success. This was going to be a dairy farm, though, so they cleared the land, fenced the paddocks and bought dozens of heads of exotic cows from Kenya. If well fed, they were known to produce much more milk than her parents' indigenous cattle had produced. Although the land had been given to Rebecca by her parents, they met a lot of opposition from squatters. They would uproot the fencing, pick quarrels and call them names. But Rebecca and Latimer persevered and the squatters realised that whether they liked it or not, the farm was going to be established. Latimer and the children helped, but it fell to Rebecca to start running the farm. The youngest of her children had now started nursery school and Rebecca thought the children would not miss her much. They hired two relatives to assist her with running with the farm: Luyombo as farm manager and Kato as his assistant. Latimer would continue his job, but the extra income would help to support their large family.

Latimer and Rebecca sold the two lorries her parents had given her and injected the money into the farm. They deliberately kept their financial worries from the children. Thankfully, they were not demanding children. Rebecca sewed most of their clothes, as her mother had done for her and her siblings. Each daughter had one 'party' dress except for the bridesmaid's dresses they had worn at weddings. Sometimes they had to share 'party' shoes; as long as they weren't going to the same party! If one of her daughters wanted a new dress, she would draw the design for her mother. Rebecca would translate it into a pattern and have the dress made before the social event occurred, no matter how busy she was on the farm. She took the time to regularly check in with each of their teachers. No matter how late she came home from the farm, she would check their homework. Any child who had not done their homework well would be woken up at 4:30 a.m. to redo it before she left at 6:30 a.m.

Rebecca always locked the house on her way out and it was eldest son Adam's duty to unlock it later. One day he said, "Mum, you have so many daughters. How come I'm the one who has to wake up and unlock the door every morning?"

"It's a man's job to open doors, chop wood, carve up the meat, pound groundnuts..." she answered. She added that his father had told her he used to do all these chores for his mother. She wasn't going to let him get out of it; it was important to Rebecca to raise her sons with respect for women.

There was no money for luxuries such as long holidays away from home, expensive toys or fancy clothes, but they made sure the children's school fees were paid and there was *always* food on the table. Latimer used to say, "You cannot study hard or do your best on an empty tummy." Feeding a large family like that meant eating a lot of fish; it was affordable and constituted what Latimer called 'brain food' which they needed 'for future reference'. He and his colleagues in the Department of Paediatrics and Child Health at Makerere University had started 'Mwanamugimu', a clinic dedicated to the prevention and treatment of severe malnourishment in children, which they believed contributed significantly to childhood diseases in the tropics.

Rebecca threw herself wholeheartedly into the work on the farm. She had always loved animals and the outdoors so it wasn't difficult. She got to know her cows by name and they would come to her when she called them, even Guy, the bull. That is, until he got over-excited one day and knocked her over. Guy was very protective of his 'ladies', especially at milking time. They restrained him a little more after that. The first year, Rebecca travelled to the farm using public transport. Her little DKW had quit working by then. There were no taxis or boda-bodas (motorcycle taxis) in the village back then, so she would take the bus from the bus park in the middle of town up to Kireka. From there, she would walk the two miles to the farm. Rebecca had always been bothered by frequent colds; that problem cleared up very quickly. Maybe the extra exercise was doing some good.

The second year, they bought a Peugeot pick-up car for Rebecca. She was one of the first two women to drive a pick-up in Kampala. Policemen would often stop the pick-up and be surprised to find a woman driving. She learnt the signals that taxi drivers used to warn each other what was on the road ahead. Rebecca was hard at work from the moment she arrived on the farm. There wasn't any task that was beneath her. She not only helped with milking the cows, cleaning the milking shed, cutting the grass and re-fencing the paddocks; she picked up special foods for the cows in her pick-up: banana peelings from hospitals and boarding schools, spent grains (dregs) from the brewery factory and elephant grass from wherever it grew wild. Some relatives would ridicule Rebecca when they found her doing menial tasks, but Rebecca was never ashamed of doing hard work for her family. She did it all with dogged determination: they were working towards their lifelong dream.

A typical day for Rebecca started at 6 a.m. when she left the children sleeping to drive to the farm. At first they had no running water on the farm. If it hadn't rained for a while, she also had to fetch water for the cows. She found the milk hands already milking the cows at 7 a.m. They loaded the milk onto the back of the pick-up and she and the driver, Kato, delivered it to the Dairy Corporation in the industrial area of Kampala. All farmers were required to support the population by selling some of their milk to the government at government price. Rebecca made sure she was home for lunch every day so that she could interact with the children. After lunch, Rebecca drove to Nsambya Hospital and Nabisunsa Girls High School where they loaded the back of the pick-up with banana peelings. She regularly supplied the girls' school with milk. It was Mr. Kaddu, a friend of her father's, who had approached the hospital about giving her their banana peelings. Three times a week, Rebecca headed to the brewery factory at Luzira to pick up their spent grains.

Rebecca would also take the time to check on her mother every day. Mulawa was only two miles down the road from the farm. By the time Rebecca got back to the farm, the afternoon milking session would be in progress. She distributed the milk from the afternoon session to her customers all around the city of Kampala: Kireka, Nabisunsa, Kyambogo, Kololo, Kamwokya, Makerere, Nakulabye, Mengo, Rubaga. She could get almost three times the government price from her regular customers. It was a rare day when Rebecca got home before eleven pm. There she would find her daughter, Bessie, waiting up for her. When she asked her why, she replied, "Mummy, someone has to wait up for you."

Chapter Thirteen

Coup D'etat

The year 1969 promised to be an eventful year. Pope Paul VI was coming to visit Uganda in July of that year. It was an exciting event for all Ugandans, Catholics as well as Protestants. The impetus for his visit was to honour the forty-five Christian martyrs who were executed by the order of Kabaka Mwanga II, in 1886, for refusing to renounce their faith. Rebecca's grandfather, Tefiro Kisosonkole, had donated the land on which the Protestant Martyr's church was built. Legend had it that he had first collected the ashes of those who had been martyred for their faith and interred them in a tomb now lying beneath the altar. The Catholic Church later bought the land next to the Protestant shrine and built their own more spectacular martyr's shrine.

Pope Paul VI met with the president of Uganda, Milton Obote, and spoke to the parliament. He visited the Catholic faithful in Rubaga Cathedral and also met with members of the Anglican Church and the Islamic Faith. He visited several hospitals and Latimer himself met the pope when he visited the Paediatric wing of Mulago Hospital. Finally, he came to the Uganda Protestant and Catholic Martyrs' Shrines in Namugongo, the site of most of the infamous executions. Anticipation of this event had meant the tarmacking of the road from Kireka to Namugongo. It passed right by Latimer and Rebecca's farm. That was a recipe for a big mess during the rainy season, but easy access to the farm for years after that.

The next major event came as an announcement over the airwaves on a grey November day: *the Kabaka had died in exile*. They said it was most likely alcohol poisoning; that he had become a poor, sad and lonely man since his exile three years earlier. The news sent shockwaves across the kingdom. Because of the political climate, his body could not be brought home to be buried properly and he was to be buried in England. Latimer and Rebecca cried together, not for the fallen king, but for their much loved friend. All the kingdoms of Uganda had been abolished by President Milton Obote in 1967 when he took over the executive powers. He wasn't being facetious when he said, "A good Muganda is a dead one." While the rest of the world was celebrating man having landed on the moon, their world was growing darker.

The following month there was an attempt on the life of the President. More imprisonments followed. Milton Obote did not proceed to summarily execute those who were arrested, though. Latimer's brother-in-law, Ephraim, and his nephew, Dan, were still in prison. Latimer still had his job, but in his position as the leading Paediatrician, he was feeling increasing pressure. One day when the president's child was ill and Latimer was summoned to the state house, he wisely chose to spend the night watching over the child than to risk taking him to hospital. He couldn't afford the liability of someone else's mistake. For Rebecca and the rest of the family, life continued its cycle: it was not the end of the world. And where there is life, there is always hope.

There was cautious optimism when President Milton Obote was overthrown by General Idi Amin on January 25, 1971. At first, no one was sure what the overnight gunfire meant.

Latimer drove the children to school and Rebecca drove to the farm as on any other day. The roads were largely deserted. She and son, Adam, were driving along Jinja Road when they came to a patchy area of fog near Kyambogo. They slowed down. Suddenly, out of the gloom appeared a group of soldiers standing in the middle of the road with guns cocked, ready to shoot. They couldn't see who was in the pick-up because of the bright headlights. Coming around to the driver's window, they encountered Rebecca. They badgered Rebecca with questions about where she was coming from and where she was going. She kept repeating the same thing: "I am going to my farm; that's where my heart is; you are just looking at a body." The soldiers were surprised at her bravery and escorted them to Kireka.

On their return journey, they had to dodge some more soldiers. When they arrived at the Dairy Corporation, the manager was surprised. He said, "You are unbelievable, Mrs. Musoke. While everyone else is running away, you have managed to get your milk through! You are a very brave woman."

The coup meant the release of Latimer's nephew and brother-in-law from prison and the return of a semblance of normal family life. Latimer flew off to the USA, alone this time, to pursue a diploma in Maternal and Child Health. While he was away, Rebecca continued to run the farm with eldest son, Adam. However, tick-borne diseases (such as East Coast Fever) were killing many of their livestock, despite regularly spraying the animals with parasiticidal agents. The government was offering farmers subsidies on the building of cattle dips for tick control. Upon Latimer's return, their friend Mr. Kanabi Nsubuga facilitated their obtaining a farmer's grant. They had already installed an electric pump to bring water up to the farm from the pond in the valley below. Now they built a cattle dip. Their livestock started thriving. For the younger children, the farm was like a big playground fitted with a cattle crush they could climb and large troughs they could swim in. They would bring their friends over to play with them. Each child had their own cow that they kept an eye on. They were so excited when their own cow gave birth to a calf.

Staying in touch with family and friends became even more important now. Latimer's sister, Marion, had moved out of town to a village in Bugerere. Latimer suggested to Rebecca that they take the children to visit her. They piled the children into the Mercedes-Benz and set off along Jinja Road. It was a long, winding, dusty ride from the tarmacked main road to her house, but they made it. The children's aunt was overjoyed to see them and prepared a special meal. While they were there, there was a heavy downpour. They all huddled inside her little house and listened to the raindrops pattering distinctly on the corrugated iron roof. After lunch, they all piled back into the car again and headed back to town. What a difference a few hours make! It was no longer raining, but there were large puddles of stagnant water every few yards, in and out of which the Mercedes' tyres had to manoeuvre. Some muddy areas it came out of easily, others sent the car slipping and sliding from side to side. More than once, the older children were instructed to get out and push the car. Finally, after falling into one pothole after another, they heard a loud shuddering noise from the bottom of the car!

Latimer stopped the car and they all got out to survey the damage. It was a sight previously unseen by them. The exhaust pipe had dropped off a few yards back and the petrol tank was hanging down, partially on the ground, with petrol freely flowing out of it. It was a good thing they had stopped when they did! Latimer quickly instructed the bystanders to bring a basin from a nearby house so that their precious fuel would not be wasted. Latimer and Rebecca instructed the children to begin walking to the main road while they figured out what to do next. The children were enjoying the adventure and took off down the road excitedly. Along the way, they picked up a straggler; a young man from the village who wouldn't leave them alone and kept insisting that they *must* see the village's famous 'marvellous hillock'. They were still anticipating this historic find when a more amusing sight caught their attention: their father being carried by on the back of a bicycle!

Latimer insisted that he had ridden a bicycle often in his youth, but that was news to the children. He bought a rope at the local shop and took it back to where the car had broken down. The children continued their trek edged on by the local 'tour guide' until they reached the landmark he had described. It turned out to be a large, smooth mound of rock jutting out of the ground; somewhat of a let-down for the would-be explorers. A little while later, the children looked up to see their mother carefully manoeuvring the Mercedes down the road while the men pushed from behind. They had used the rope to secure the petrol tank back into the chassis of the car and were able to reach the main road safely. They sputtered along until they reached the first petrol station. The mechanic inspected the engine, cleaned it out and told them they were good to go, despite the unorthodox fixtures and missing exhaust pipe.

Things were looking up and Latimer and Rebecca decided to invest in the children's broader education as well as their schooling. They often took them to the botanical gardens in Entebbe but warned them not to step into the waters of Lake Victoria, for fear of bilharzia (schistosomiasis). They would also take them to visit the Entebbe zoo. Once, they put the children on a train to Jinja, just for the fun of it, while they and eldest son Adam drove the car to meet them there. The following year, Latimer and Rebecca were able to send Adam to study in England. Henry returned from the United States after completing his studies and became a professor in the engineering department at Makerere University.

By 1973, Latimer and Rebecca had enough money saved to take the children on a short holiday. They were celebrating

Latimer being made a Professor and Head of the Department of Paediatrics at Makerere University. They travelled west through Masaka, Mbarara, Kabale and Fort Portal before returning home. Sometimes they stayed in hotels, sometimes with friends. The highlight was the trip to the Queen Elizabeth National Park and Mweya Safari Lodge. They got to see the wild animals in their natural habitat, not just in the zoo. It was a trip the children talked about for years afterwards.

Chapter Fourteen

Changing Times

President Amin had endeared himself to the Baganda when he permitted the return of the late Kabaka's body for a proper burial in the ancestral tombs at Kasubi Nabulagala. The Kabaka's body was laid in state at Namirembe Cathedral first. Latimer and Rebecca were among the mourners who attended the viewing. When she reached the coffin, Rebecca said to herself: 'It really is him.' Many had not wanted to believe it until they saw the physical evidence. The Kabaka was laid to rest in the Kasubi Tombs next to his forefathers: Ssekabaka Mutesa I, Ssekabaka Mwanga II and Ssekabaka Chwa II. At the death of his father, fourteen-year-old Ronald Muwenda Mutebi, heir designate, had performed the required ritual that symbolised the passing of the torch – laying a special bark cloth over his father's body. He accompanied the body of his late father back to Uganda on March 30, 1971.

As required by custom, Ronald was born in Buganda and educated briefly at Budo Junior School before moving to England when his father was exiled. Rebecca's parents held a feast for Crown Prince Ronald Muwenda Mutebi in their home during his brief return. Her youngest children had never witnessed the era of the kingdom. When they saw their cousin, they whispered to their mother, "Do we have to kneel?"

Ronnie overheard them and smiled to himself. However, the kingdoms were not reinstated and the crown prince returned to England to continue his studies – still a crown prince. His Mengo palace remained occupied by Amin's soldiers – still a military barracks.

It wasn't long, however, before the optimism born out of the regime change turned to fear and dread as prominent citizens began disappearing. The expulsion of the Asians in 1972 was quickly followed by the exodus of most of the Europeans. Rebecca had many friends and customers among the Indians who were forced to leave, yet not a single one left without paying their debt. They offered her some of the property they were being forced to abandon, but Rebecca declined most of it. She was never one to accept hand-outs, believing as she did in the rewards of honest, hard work. They bought a piano for the children from one departing family. The European expatriates who worked with Latimer and were friends as well as colleagues were finding the political climate increasingly hostile. It was clear that Al-Hajji, Field Marshall Dr. Idi Amin Dada, VC, DSO, MC, CBE had no respect for anyone, educated or uneducated. His antics were turning Uganda into a caricature and the laughing stock of the world. Meanwhile, they were slowly being isolated from the rest of the world economically and inflation was going through the roof.

Latimer was doctor to President Idi Amin's children, but he didn't feel safe. Some of the people disappearing were his colleagues and prominent members of the community. The targets appeared to be random, from every tribe, but this did not ease his apprehension. Rebecca watched as the brilliant, self-confident, ambitious young man she had married became increasingly frustrated. There were no longer adequate personnel in the department; medical supplies and equipment were in short supply; the medical school was no longer recognised by the British Medical Society and the Ugandan children he had dedicated his life to were dying of curable diseases. He had always been a social drinker, but alcohol increasingly became his place of solace. She would try to lift his spirits by reminding him of all the blessings they had: all their children were healthy, well-behaved and doing well in school; with the farm turning a profit, they were doing much better financially; and they still had each other as well as a supportive family. She would also remind him of his own oft-repeated motto: "Life is built on confidence." The words seemed to fall on deaf ears.

Early in 1974, Rebecca discovered that her cousin, Sarah Kabejja, the mother of Crown Prince Ronald Mutebi, had been diagnosed with breast cancer. When Rebecca went to see her at Mulago Hospital, she had already been to England once for treatment and returned. Her doctors were now telling the family that there was nothing more they could do for her in Uganda; she should return to England for further treatment. They said goodbye to her wondering if they would ever see her alive again. They did not. She passed away in England in August 1974 and her body was brought home for burial. When they first heard the news of her passing away, the whole family gathered at her home in Nakasero. She had been given an official residence there by President Idi Amin. Afterwards, the wake was moved to her father's home in Banda. Rebecca and the rest of the family went to Banda and started making preparations for the arrival of the body. Rebecca looked at her cousin's body as she lay in the coffin and thought, 'She looks beautiful lying there in her busuti; just as if she was sleeping.' They buried her next to her mother in the family graveyard at Kyaliwajjala as she had requested in her will. Her will did not name a successor.

Latimer was initially pleased when Rebecca was nominated by her family as heir to her cousin, Sarah. Perhaps he thought it would be their way of paying tribute to their fallen king. He wasn't aware of the deep rifts that had developed in Rebecca's family long before he joined it. When her uncle suggested her name, Rebecca's father vehemently opposed it on her behalf. He told the family that they had not raised their daughter in the traditions of the palace; how could she be expected to fulfil them? *She* wished the ground could swallow her up, or at least if she could run away. How could she be **heir to the queen mother (Namasole)**; the woman who had given birth to the future king? She was just an ordinary, hardworking housewife and farmer, but she was happy. Culturally, she could not raise her objections, but Rebecca couldn't help but remember when, as a young girl, she first became aware of the family feud. Prior to that time, it felt like one big, happy, close-knit family. She and her brothers always looked forward to the monthly visits to one or the other of their aunt's or uncle's homes for the family get-together. Their own home was a popular spot because of mother's talents. But after the feud began, Rebecca saw less and less of her cousins.

Rebecca had written to her uncle back then, addressing him as 'Taata omuto' (my young father) and begging him to resolve the conflict between himself and her own father. His reply was brutal in its honesty and sarcasm and deeply painful to the sensitive young girl who was trying to repair the breach in the family. She also remembered how his new wife had insisted that Rebecca's father relinquish the Kisosonkole name when her stepdaughter married into the royal family; despite him being the firstborn. The irony of her uncle now begging her to accept the queen mother role was not lost on her. Rebecca's Uncle Christopher had only had two daughters with his first wife: one was already the Nnabagereka, so she could not be heir to her sister. The two daughters of his South African wife were considered ineligible. His brother, Kupliano, had only had two daughters as well. Rebecca's little sister, Damallie, was living too far away in England to be considered a viable option. The lot fell to Rebecca.

Her father pleaded with her aunts, saying over and over, "Becca has never been exposed to the traditions of the royal family. How is she going to fulfil this role?" She and her father acquiesced only after her aunts argued that there was no one else who could fill the role and reminded them of their duty to the family and the kingdom.

Auntie Try told her father, "When you give birth to a child, she isn't just your child. She belongs to the whole clan."

Rebecca took courage when she remembered the words of Prime Minister Nehru: never give up your culture. She said to herself, "Ekingumya, newankubadde nga ntidde, Taata wange n'owa Sarah bonna bayonka ku'beere limu, elya Damali Nalule" that is to say, "Even though I don't feel ready to take on this role, I must remember that my father and Sarah's father were nursed by the same mother, Damali Nalule." She responded, "If the family is confident that no one but I should inherit the role of queen mother, I will submit; and God will help me to fulfil my duty."

Crown Prince Ronnie did not get to attend his mother's funeral, but President Idi Amin did, to everyone's surprise. Even though the kingdom had not been restored, Ronnie was now unofficially the Kabaka. The Kabaka neither mourns the dead, nor attends funerals. He joined them for the ceremonies afterwards. They made Rebecca sit on a special piece of bark cloth (lubugo) and then began telling her what her duties would be as the heir to the queen mother. Her head started spinning as the admonishments went on and on; some things she had never even heard of. Crown Prince Ronald Muwenda Mutebi and his brother, Richard Walugembe, were instructed to sit on her lap and told, "This is your mother from now on." The ceremonies continued all night long. Finally, just before dawn, they ended up at the Kasubi Tombs, the king's ancestral burial grounds.

She and the crown prince were welcomed with much traditional drumming and dancing. Then he was whisked away to perform his ceremonial duties, and she went on to perform hers as the Namasole. One ritual involved her being chased with a spear by one of the 'concubines' who lived at Kasubi. All 'concubines' of the former kings had heirs who were designated caretakers of the tombs. In the olden days, if the Namasole was caught, she would be killed. It meant that the kings who were buried there did not accept her. Rebecca didn't have any trouble outrunning the 'concubine'. Her days racing with her brothers weren't for nothing. By the time they caught up with Rebecca, she had exited the compound. In another ritual, Rebecca had to run through a waterfall and emerge into some caves. She had no idea of the depth of the cascading water, but her days in the swimming pool helped her get through that test.

The next day, they drove her to Bamunanika Palace where more ceremonies were performed. Because Rebecca's father was the head of his line of the clan, a week later she was taken to meet the heads of the Nkima (monkey) clan she belonged to. She was officially introduced to the clan elders: first to Mugogo, then Kinyolo, then Mugema. At each location, they had to deliver gifts to the elders.

Before Rebecca's new royal 'son' returned to England, she invited him to their home in Makerere. Adam had come home from England for a short holiday as well. Other attendees were shocked when Adam casually sat down on the arm of the armchair in which the crown prince was sitting. He and Adam had become friends by now; he had taken Adam to see his mother while she was still hospitalised in England. Rebecca did not get a chance to spend much personal time with the crown prince. She was given a brief introduction to his late mother's friend and confidante, Rose Kibaya, and his guardian, Captain Owen, with whom she was able to keep in touch. Rebecca *was* able to spend some time with his younger brother, Richard, and she did her best to comfort him on the loss of his mother. He was only eighteen years old and cried uncontrollably at the funeral and during the ceremonies. The crown prince himself did not show any emotion; he had been groomed not to show any sign of weakness in front of his subjects.

Chapter Fifteen

Accidents

The political and economic situation continued to deteriorate under President Idi Amin. The hijacking of the Air France plane by Palestinian terrorists given asylum by Idi Amin, followed by the successful Israeli raid on Entebbe Airport to free the hostages, did nothing to improve Uganda's image. Neither did the beating of the Makerere University students on Black Monday by Amin's soldiers in that same year. Nor did the murder of Archbishop Janani Luwum the following year. There was a massive exodus of Ugandans to other parts of the world, including Rebecca's brother, Arnold, the dentist. Latimer considered leaving, too. He had often been offered jobs with the World Health Organization; but he did not want to uproot his family again. His two eldest daughters, Eva and Harriet, were getting married, as did two of Rebecca's brothers, Myers and Tempora. Their other older children were in the university; the younger ones were in high school. Adam had come home for one visit but did not return for the next five years. He needed the family to stay together.

Latimer's drinking was progressing. His only other solace was his favourite classical music that he listened to for hours at a time. Sometimes, he would wake the children up in the middle of the night for them to listen to Beethoven or Mozart. Rebecca had learnt to sleep through it; she had an early start most days. The best she could do was pray for him and give him her loving support. When he rang and said he needed a ride home from the bar, she was always there; when he lost his temper and barked at everybody, Rebecca would answer him with loving patience and usually calm him down. Despite barking loud enough to make the house shake to its foundation, he was never physically abusive to her or the children. Nevertheless, it was hard for Rebecca to watch the love of her life go from an ambitious overachiever to a person of growing despondency.

One day her worst fears were realised. Latimer had gone to the farm in his Mercedes-Benz because the pick-up was being repaired. She and the lastborn, Becky, were the only two in the house. At about eleven pm, Rebecca heard a Land Rover in the driveway. She got up and went outside. The driver told her to come over quickly and check the back of the car. There was Latimer, covered in blood. Rebecca was gripped with fear, but there was no time to waste. They were taking him to Mulago Hospital and told her to follow them. Rebecca called over Latimer's eldest son, Henry, to take her to the hospital. She locked the house, jumped in the car and they raced to Mulago hospital. By the time they got there, he had already been taken to theatre where his broken hip was being repaired. It was only while sitting outside the theatre waiting that she suddenly remembered she had locked Becky in the house! They drove back home and let Rebecca's Aunt Hannah into the house to take care of her.

The car was a write-off, he had a broken leg, but thankfully, Latimer had survived. He would walk with a cane the rest of his life. Family and friends rallied around them during Latimer's three-month hospitalisation. Rebecca had to divide her time between the farm and the hospital. Her friend and neighbour, Agnes Sekabunga, agreed to take Becky into her home so that they could take her to school every day with their children. Their youngest didn't come home until Christmas. Rebecca and

Latimer came home to find their house completely overhauled and sparkling clean. It was the last act of kindness Henry performed for them before he too fled the country. Rebecca was grateful. The only problem was that there were things in her house she could not locate for years.

Rebecca had inherited a piece of land from her maternal grandmother, Zirimbuga, who passed away when she was only five years old. After Latimer's Mercedes was written off, she sold sixteen of the twenty acres she owned so that they could buy a new car. They used the money to buy a new Toyota Corolla estate car. This had not been Latimer's first car accident, but Rebecca hoped it would be his last. She remembered him telling her about a car accident that he had before they were married. He was driving from Kampala to Entebbe. At the point where Lake Victoria comes close to the main road, the road slopes downhill. Latimer somehow lost control of his car. It rolled over several times but it did not roll into the lake. He survived to tell the story. When he was given time off work to recover from his injuries, he had come to Nairobi to visit her at the Kabete School of Social Work.

Rebecca could also remember a car accident that they had survived together. It was 1965. She and Latimer were in a convoy of doctors heading upcountry to Gulu when the Volkswagen van they were in was sideswiped by another car. Before they set off, Rebecca was getting ready to sit in the middle seat next to the door. One of the European doctors said to her, "Rebecca, we cannot allow you to sit there; please move to the middle of the seat and I will sit beside you." Latimer was told to sit in the middle of the seat behind her.

Rebecca did not remember the accident itself but was told that the car veered off the road, hit the embankment, careened back to the opposite side and rolled over. She woke up to hear Latimer calling her name. She found herself lying on the roadside, wrapped in the canvas that had been covering the hatch in the roof of the van. The impact must have picked her up and ejected her straight through it, wrapping her safely in the process. Rebecca had nothing but a scratch on her hand. She and the driver were the only ones to escape without serious injury. Latimer broke his right arm in two places. The gentleman who had exchanged seats with her broke his pelvis, another gentleman broke his collarbone, another his hips, and a good friend and colleague, Professor Edgar Mannheimer, lost his life. The survivors were all taken to the nearest hospital in Hoima. There was no electricity in the hospital, only pressure lanterns. They *were* able to ring home and notify the family about the accident. The next day, they were transferred to Mulago Hospital by ambulance. The Lord who had spared their lives then was still watching over them.

Their house at Makerere was built into the side of the hill, with the driveway, garage and servant's quarters on an upper level. There were two ways to get down to the house: one, a long flight of steep steps adjacent to the house, the other, a slightly longer route down a grassy slope, then a short flight of steps to the kitchen. After his accident, Latimer had to take the longer route.

The steeper flight of stairs was infamous in its own right. One evening, Rebecca had been standing in the kitchen chatting with her brother-in-law, John Serebe, when they heard a loud thud and the house shuddered for a few seconds. They rushed outside to find Uncle John's car at a dangerous angle on the long flight of steps, with its front bumper wedged tightly into the corner of the house. His two oldest children were staring transfixed through the windscreen. His wife was still seated on the back seat. She had been nursing the baby and was lifted out of the car bewailing the fate of her children. Her husband had to reassure her over and over. Those naughty children who had let the hand brake down and allowed the car to roll over the safety bar and down the stairs were fine; just covered in egg – literally. There had been several cartons of eggs stashed on the rear deck of the car.

On January 12th, 1977, Latimer and Rebecca had a surprise feast prepared for them by the children to celebrate their 25th wedding anniversary. That year, Rebecca's mother's health began to deteriorate. She had had long-standing hypertension, which weakened her heart and gradually led to her being unable to work. She had had to have surgery to remove her thyroid gland that had become overactive. She had had to have cataract surgery to try to restore her failing eyesight. The surgery did not go well. Despite her infirm status, mother still loved to have her grandchildren over for the weekend. Since their home was not far from the farm, Rebecca could bring the children over on Friday and pick them up on Sunday. Sundays were always special, as other family members would come over to watch their favourite TV programme, 'Big Valley', and to have high tea with the delicious pastries grandmother still prepared. The grandchildren had named her 'Jjajja afuka chai' which means 'the grandparent who pours the tea.' She treasured being able to continue playing that role.

Their grandfather, the children had named 'Jjajja avuga landrova' which means 'the grandparent who drives a Land Rover. That name stuck even after he stopped driving a Land Rover and bought a different type of car. Rebecca still drove her pick-up back and forth to the farm. Now she and her father teamed up to take care of her ailing mother; taking her to doctor's appointments and waiting while she visited family and friends. Mother was in and out of hospital. She and Rebecca's father moved from their home in Mulawa to their home in Mengo so that they could be nearer the hospitals. Finally, it came to the point where Rebecca's father could no longer care for her alone, and Latimer and Rebecca had both her parents move into their home.

It wasn't a difficult decision for them to make. Latimer had lost both his parents before he asked Rebecca to marry him. His father, Yokana Kamya Bafiirawala, a Ssaza (county) chief, had died while he was still in school. His mother, Louise Nawolida

Nakku, had died when he was already a medical doctor, but he was living too far away to help her. Rebecca's parents had treated him like a son and had been there to support them through all their highs and lows. It was during this time, however, that Rebecca really missed having her sister, Damallie, nearby. Damallie had followed in their father's footsteps and graduated from college in England with a teaching degree. She had stayed on in England to begin her teaching career and was adored by all her pupils. She had that natural ability to bring out the best in her pupils while maintaining discipline and making learning fun. Damallie visited frequently from England, but her longest holiday was only five weeks long, so she could provide only limited physical comfort. She was invaluable, though, with her moral support, writing letters to Rebecca regularly and frequently.

Moving her parents into their home was not without controversy. For a husband to have his in-laws living under the same roof is not culturally acceptable, and Rebecca knew tongues were wagging across the aisle. Even if there had been nursing care homes in Kampala at that time, Latimer and Rebecca would not have dreamt of abandoning her mother to one. Rebecca wished that her brothers would chip in and help out, but she discovered that brothers just aren't inclined that way. One of her sisters-in-law was kind enough to provide meals when Rebecca had to stay at the hospital with her mother. Rebecca thanked God every day that He had given her so many daughters. Two of them were already in medical school and providing invaluable support to her.

Late in 1978, Rebecca wrote to her sister in England, telling her that their mother was very ill and that she may not survive until her next summer holiday. She suggested that Damallie come and see her mother that Christmas.

Chapter Sixteen

Hope Deferred

The year 1979 started with the rumour of a war to liberate Uganda from the dictator, Idi Amin. Ironically, Rebecca had met the man himself one day when she was going to visit her mother in hospital. She was standing in front of the lift when the door opened and there he was! Rebecca recognised him immediately and being taken aback, she took a step backwards. He said, "Please, madam, get in the lift; we are both going to see patients." While riding in the lift, he asked Rebecca whom she was there to see. Rebecca told him she was there to see her mother who was in the critical care ward, 3D. She got off the lift on the third floor and left him going up. A short while later, Rebecca was at her mother's bedside when she looked up to see the president entering her mother's ward. He came straight over to them, asked kindly after her mother and then, wishing her a speedy recovery, he left. Rebecca was too astonished to say anything for several minutes.

In March of that year, the different factions of Ugandan exiles fighting for its liberation met in Moshi, Tanzania. The 'Moshi Conference' was held from 23rd March to 26th March, 1979 under the leadership of President Julius Nyerere of Tanzania. At the conference, the Uganda National Liberation Front (UNLF) was born. It combined the different military factions. On the political front, a government-in-exile led by Professor Yusufu Lule was elected. The advancing Tanzania People's Defence forces (TPDF), aided by the UNLF, had begun marching from the southern Uganda/Tanzania border in late 1978. After the conference, the war progressed very quickly. They were welcomed by people all along the way. A new system of governance, based on the 'Mayumba Kumi' system (a leader for every ten houses) used in Tanzania was set up in each town that was liberated. Information on the progress of the war was disseminated daily by 'Radio Katwe' and there was a general air of excitement and expectancy as people huddled over their radios every evening, usually in the dark, to catch the latest news. The decisive battle at Lukaya, 100 kilometres from Kampala, broke Amin's hold on power and he fled eastwards.[4]

Rebecca had her parents in her house at Makerere and most of the children were either on the university campus, the Mulago Hospital campus or in boarding school. There was a curfew from dusk 'til dawn. They continued to live their daily lives in Kampala as best they could, with the dwindling supplies and the overarching threat of war. Rebecca would drive to the village through numerous military roadblocks to fetch food. On the way back, she had to give up some of the food to the soldiers so that they would let her through. They got to know her very well, even warning her to take extra food one day because the 'guerrillas' were getting close. The muffled sounds of mortar and bombs hitting the ground were moving closer from the west every day. Rebecca learnt to hide her fear as she confronted the soldiers every day. Little did she know that it was just a dress rehearsal for future, more terrifying confrontations with armed men in uniform.

Everyone was talking about the 'Saba Saba' (Ballistic Missile Launcher) which could hit a target many kilometres away. Eventually, the sounds of the war were close enough that shrapnel was hitting rooftops nearby. One day, there was a particularly loud bang that sounded like a something had exploded close to the other side of the house. Latimer and Rebecca ran quickly over to mother's room, afraid that with her weak heart, the shock might have been too much for her. She was all right. That day, Latimer went shopping and bought a bottle of embalming fluid. He said, "If something happens to Mama while we are here and we cannot get to the village to bury her, we shall bury her right here in the compound. When things get better, we can always exhume her body and take it to the village."

A few days later, there was a report that the Cancer Institute at Mulago had been hit by a bomb. That's where her two medical student daughters, Louise and Philippa, were staying. There were no mobile phones in those days and no way to reach them. Rebecca walked from their home at Makerere to Mulago, two kilometres away, wending her way through debris all along the road to check on her daughters. She saw houses that had been hit and was told about casualties, but she kept on going. She smelled the terrible stench of death as she passed by the Mulago mortuary that had already filled up. All she could do was pray. She reached her daughter's housing and found them safe. Although a building near the Cancer Institute had been hit, theirs had not. They eagerly recounted their story of survival; how they had hidden under their beds, terrified and prayed as the bombing took place all around them. Rebecca and her daughters thanked God for His protection, but it was a sad time because one of their colleagues had been killed.

It was rumoured that Makerere was going to be the next target of the invading army. Rebecca felt that the safest place for the two youngest children was at their boarding school in Gayaza, twenty kilometres north of the city. She was thankful that the headmistress had chosen to keep the school open throughout the war. She and Headmistress Miss Sheelagh Warren had become well acquainted when she asked Rebecca to join the school's agriculture committee. Rebecca's other children told her they would fend for themselves. Her son, Wilfred, suggested that she move their father and their grandparents to a safer location. Their house near the main entrance of the university campus was probably not the safest place. It was time to make a prayerful decision.

The Toyota Corolla was sitting idle in the garage. In these perilous times, you did not keep a car with tyres on it or a full tank of petrol sitting in your driveway. It was liable to disappear. Rebecca and her son replaced the tyres on the car and she began to prepare her parents for the trip. She planned to drive her husband and parents to the village where she expected they would be safer. Wilfred and his friends had already begun the twenty-kilometre trek to the offsite campus of the university north of the city. But ... Latimer adamantly refused to go anywhere. Rebecca had no choice but to drive her parents over to one of the university halls on the opposite side of the campus. The children's cousin, Joanna Kamanyi, occupied a flat on the ground floor there. She arranged a room for Rebecca's parents to spend the night in the basement with their granddaughter. Rebecca headed back home. Not even the threat of annihilation would make her break her vows to her husband. She, Latimer and his sister, Marion, hunkered down at home and waited for the outcome of the battle for Kampala.

The news came on the radio early on the morning of April 14th. The Uganda National Liberation Army, with the assistance of the TPDF, had been victorious and successfully deposed the despot, Idi Amin. He was on the run and so were his soldiers, some of whom Rebecca met fleeing when she drove to the farm later that day. There were also signs that the battle the night before had been fierce, especially around Radio Uganda and on the golf course where there were several dead bodies lying unattended. But there was jubilation throughout the city. People came out of their houses to welcome the conquerors; even Latimer came out and greeted them in Swahili, "Habari". The air of optimism was everywhere. Riots and looting followed soon after that, but no one cared. The new government under Professor Yusufu Lule would replace everything and do much, much more. Not only had Rebecca's prayers been answered: her husband, her children and her parents were all safe; but her brother, Dr. Arnold Bisase, had returned with the conquerors as the Minister of Health.

It was a surprise to them all, but especially wonderful for her ailing mother. She had last seen her son five years earlier and despaired of seeing him again in this lifetime. His prominent position in the new government even gave Latimer hope for the future. His countenance was different and he was once again making plans at work and for the farm. It was as if the world had discovered a new star. For Rebecca, that was all the blessing she needed. But her mother said to her brother, "Son, unless you're bringing back the Europeans, I don't see any future in this coup." Her brother laughed. He was excited to be home and believed in the power of the coalition government. They were going to restore Uganda to its former glory as the 'Pearl of Africa'!

No one should despise the prophetic wisdom of an old woman. The jubilation lasted only two months. The rest of the country hadn't even been completely liberated before there was another change in leadership. President Yusufu Lule was removed by a vote of no confidence from the National Consultative Council (N.C.C). He was replaced by the lesser-known Godfrey Binaisa. The people poured out into the streets in protest, shouting "Twagala Lule! Oba tuffa, tuffe!" ("We want Lule! Even if it means death!"). But the uprising was quickly quelled and people slowly began to accept the reality that their 'saviour', President Lule, was not coming back.

A tangible depression settled over the land as thick as the darkness on a moonless night. Rebecca's mother's health took a turn for the worse and she was admitted to the critical care ward at Mulago Hospital again. Her once jubilant son came to visit her at 6:30 a.m. one morning. He put on a brave face for his mother and tried to look positive, but she knew. She said, "You've come to say goodbye." He protested that he had only come to pay her a visit, but when he and Rebecca went out of the room, he told Rebecca that he was indeed leaving. He had been summoned to the state house in Entebbe, but someone had tipped him off that the outcome of the meeting may not be good. He gave Rebecca some final instructions and then they hugged each other goodbye.

Chapter Seventeen

Death in the Family

The next two months, Rebecca was in and out of hospital with her mother. At one point, the doctors went on strike because so many of their colleagues had been killed. Although access to the critical care unit was normally restricted, the family was given special concession. Many relatives were coming to the hospital to help now. Rebecca was at her mother's bedside to make sure she got the very best nursing care. Her father was close beside his wife, wiping her forehead, speaking lovingly to her and firmly believing that she would walk out of the hospital one day. But mother was getting weaker every day. When she could still speak, she gave Rebecca specific instructions about her father's needs: what to feed him, how to dress him. She always paid attention to every detail that concerned him. She had been his lifelong confidante and the rock in the winds of life's storms. Her advice had spared him trouble countless times in their life together. They had celebrated 50 years of marriage in March of that very year; but the bond of their love was not just golden, it was a solid diamond, the envy of all who knew them.

Rebecca's daughters would take turns taking care of their grandmother. The last two days of her life, she was comatose. On one of those days, the girls came to the hospital room and sang her favourite hymn for her: *'Yesu, bulijjo nkwetaga, Tondeka bwomu; Beera nange Gwe okumpi, So tonvamu'* which means, 'Jesus, I need you every day, don't leave me alone; Stay close to me, I pray; do not forsake me'. She nodded her head slowly as they sang and they were sure they saw a tear in her eye when they finished the last verse. Although mother had been ill for so long, almost ten years, it was hard for Rebecca to let her go. She had said to Rebecca on this final admission, "Becca, you have looked after me these eight years and I have been in and out of hospital, but this is the last time. I will never come back home alive." Even though Rebecca suspected in the back of her mind that her mother was right, she didn't want to believe it.

She was the one who had instilled every lasting value in her. She could hear her words of advice echoing down through the decades: love your husband and your children; forgive each other; joy and sorrow will come but persevere; remember that things will change. No husband should have a shirt missing a button or a hole in his sock; that's your responsibility. Be thankful. Remember those who are worse off than you; pray for the poor; always give to the needy. Give honour to others if you want honour given back to you. Always greet people and refer to them as 'Ssebo'(Sir) and 'Nnyabo' (Madam). When you visit, wait to be seated; when you are served, don't take seconds unless everyone else has eaten. Treat your in-laws well; they are your children's aunts and uncles. If anything happens to you, they're the ones who will take care of your children. Treat all your servants well. Always wear clean underwear; you never know when you'll be in an accident...

It was from her mother that Rebecca had inherited her deep sense of right and wrong. Rebecca couldn't stand injustice of any sort. On one occasion during Idi Amin's regime, she was driving with her eldest son near the Queen's Clock Tower when they witnessed an accident. A military man in a jeep came racing down the hill and passed them. Another car was reversing into the road and the jeep was going too fast to avoid hitting it. Although it was the army driver's fault, he jumped out of his jeep and started trying to beat up the other poor man. Rebecca wanted to get out of her car and confront the army man. It was all her son could do to restrain her. On another occasion, Rebecca had just taken her two youngest daughters back to boarding school at Gayaza High School. It was Becky's first day but she wasn't at a loss for company. She and several of her schoolmates from Nakasero were gathered together chattering away. One little girl in their dormitory, who was not from the same primary school, was standing to the side, too shy to join in the conversation. Rebecca stepped forward and said to the excited group of girls, "This is wrong; you need to include this girl, too. Why don't you all introduce yourselves?"

Mother's passing away that 5th day of August was quiet. Rebecca watched as she simply stopped breathing and the monitors went quiet. She had sent her father back to his room on the sixth floor with Auntie Joyce Kanyerezi to get some rest. Auntie Joyce was a nurse on the hospital staff. His friend, Mr. Naluma, was also with him. The doctor had prescribed him a sleeping tablet. Mother's nurse tried to encourage Rebecca to go and get some rest too, but she wouldn't go. Then she suggested that they go and get some tea, but Rebecca would not leave her mother's side. The nurse had just left the room when the monitors went quiet, so Rebecca was alone with her mother. Rebecca knelt down and prayed over her departed mother, that God would rest her soul in peace. She prayed for strength for herself, that she would be able to care for both her husband and her father. When the nurse came back, Rebecca told her that her mother had passed away. She had to check for herself. She couldn't believe that it had happened so quickly.

Rebecca and the nurse bathed and dressed her mother's body. Then she went to look for her father. She gently broke the news to him that mother had gone. They came back to her room. She looked so lovely; just as if she was asleep. Her husband kissed her for the last time, then he and Rebecca knelt down together and prayed; thanking God for her life and the precious gift she had been to both of them. Rebecca took her father back to the sixth floor so that others could come and pay their respects. She did not wail aloud like some of her relatives, but she could feel the emptiness growing deep in her belly. There's something about knowing that the woman who gave you life is no longer living. It sucks the life out of you. She had to be strong for the rest of the family, though. There were funeral arrangements to be made and she wanted to make sure her sister could make it back from England in time for the funeral. The children had to come home from school; others would have to take over the duties of the farm.

It was about 2 a.m. when Rebecca got back to their room on the sixth floor. She was so exhausted that she promptly fell asleep. When she awoke at 6 a.m., she noticed that her father was not in his bed. No one knew where he had gone, but Mr. Naluma thought that perhaps he had returned to his dearly departed wife's side. Rebecca's father and Mr. Naluma were close; they had toured Uganda together on their bicycles back in the 1930s. The nurse on duty confirmed that he had indeed returned and sat beside his wife's body for a while, but that had been hours ago. They searched for him for the next several hours with increasing anxiety that the death of his wife had put him over the edge and he had decided to end his own life. He was nowhere to be found. Rebecca drove the short distance home and picked up Latimer. On their return, they were informed that an elderly gentleman had been found stuck in a lift. They were still trying to extricate him.

Rebecca's poor father had entered a lift when he left the critical care ward on the third floor to return to the sixth floor. He was unaware that the lift was broken. The doors closed, the lift went up a short distance and then stopped between floors. He pushed several buttons but nothing happened. He called for help but soon realised no one would hear him; it was the middle of the night. He leaned against the side of the lift, but he must have eventually passed out from exhaustion. He had smashed his teeth in the process. It was such a relief when they finally found him, groggy and disoriented from pain and grief. He was promptly admitted to hospital for his injuries and only left there to attend his wife's funeral. Rebecca had to leave him in the care of her eldest daughter, Damallie, while she went to start making the funeral arrangements.

After the funeral service in their church at Kira, mother was laid to rest at the family gravesite in Kyaliwajjala, next to her husband's parents. Little sister, Damallie, caught the earliest flight she could get from London but did not make it in time for the funeral. She was forever grateful that Rebecca had advised her to come home at Christmas and see her mother while she was still alive. Life was never the same for their father after he lost his beloved wife, Damali. He was in hospital recovering from his injuries for several weeks. Rebecca and Damallie asked him to write his and their mother's love story, but he insisted that he could not remember anything. The memories were too painful. Well-meaning people who told him, "Better to have loved and lost than never to have loved at all" didn't know what they were talking about. The sun never shined as bright again, roses never again smelled as sweet, favourite foods no longer tasted as good and music they had shared became unbearable to listen to. His faith in God was the only thing keeping him alive.

After her mother passed away, Rebecca tried to get back to her regular routine. Her brother, Arnold, suggested that she bring their father to Mombasa to recuperate. He thought the break would be good for her too. Her father was reluctant to go, but Rebecca edged him on with the words, "Dad, we love you so much. Mum's work was done; you haven't finished yours. Please keep doing yours, otherwise Mum will not be happy with you." She started making preparations for them to travel, but she and

Latimer both thought it was a good idea if they held mother's last funeral rites before they left. It would help to bring them all closure. With the ever-changing political climate, you didn't want to leave loose ends hanging for too long. The collapse of Professor Lule's government, which had briefly brought so much hope, had chopped the legs off a society that was already tottering. Those who, like Latimer, had been revived by the glimmer of hope... lapsed back into despondency.

Rebecca was getting ready to drive her two youngest daughters back to boarding school that August. Their father came out to say goodbye. He told the girls, "Next year is going to be a difficult year for your mother. Make sure you study hard and pass your exams. Bessie, you must make it to the university. Becky, you must make it to senior five. I will not be there for you if you don't pass your exams." Nobody understood what he meant; he had always been there for them as far as their schooling was concerned. Always there to encourage them with a loud, "Congulakulaaations!" when they did pass their exams. And when they didn't do as well, telling them they would do better next time. He liked to say, "You'll beat them!"

Chapter Eighteen

Blindsided

It was going to be a busy few days. On October 5th, Rebecca went to the village to prepare for her mother's last funeral rites. The function took place the following day. Mother had chosen one of her granddaughters to be her heir, but the clan vetoed it and chose Rebecca's cousin, Eva Njuki. With the ceremonies completed, Latimer and the children returned home that evening. Latimer stopped by the farm on his way home. Rebecca returned home the following day after the clean-up was completed. Latimer's brother, Cranimer, was there visiting his brother. Rebecca was happy to find him there keeping Latimer company. After tea, Rebecca drove him home, then stopped by her sister-in-law's house to pick up some plates and cutlery. Eldest daughter Damallie was graduating from the university the next day with a degree in Electrical Engineering. The house was full of well-wishers, and the ladies who had come to cook for the graduation party were already there. Rebecca and the girls were ironing their clothes for the next day. She asked Latimer which suit he was going to wear. His reply was, "I may not come to the graduation." She knew he couldn't be serious. It was going to be a proud moment for both of them.

The youngest girls were home from boarding school because of the Independence Day holiday. The 7th of October was Becky's sweet sixteenth birthday and they stayed up to sing her 'Happy Birthday' at 11:30 p.m., the time of her birth. That night, Rebecca and the girls sat up late talking about their late grandmother and their father. They were grateful for the life of their loving grandmother and still had hope for their father. They talked about what they could do to encourage him and they prayed for him, fervently hoping that God would turn things around. They did not know how little time they had left with him.

After praying with her daughters, Rebecca returned to her bedroom where she found Latimer awake. He was hungry, so she brought him some milk and sausages. She remembered that the girls had said he had refused to eat anything during the day. He asked for a cigarette and she brought it to him. He was unusually communicative that night. He said, "Mama Becca, you have taken such good care of me; I'm going to tell my mother." Then he added, "I've been a difficult man, but you have persevered; you have won the battle and God will reward you." Rebecca tried to keep the mood light, but he went on to repeat what he had told the children: "Becca, next year will be a difficult year for you."

She asked him, "Why just for me? What about you?" Only half serious, she said to him, "If I were left alone, I would ask God for two things: first that I would be able survive on my own. I don't want another man in my life. Secondly, I would ask God for a widow's purse, so that I would be able to educate the children."

Latimer asked Rebecca to help him to the toilet. As she did, she reminded him how he used to escort her to the outhouse when they first got married, because she was afraid of the dark. He laughed. He returned from the toilet and lay down. That's when Rebecca noticed that he was sweating. In concern, she asked him what was wrong and what she could do to make him feel better. He asked for a cool cloth on his forehead and she fetched it. She decided to give him a sponge bath as well. Then she changed his pyjamas. When she touched his feet, she noticed that they were cold. That's when she really became concerned and suggested she ring the doctor. Latimer said, "No, I'll see the doctor in the morning." Rebecca decided to call the doctor anyway. His breathing didn't sound right. It was 4 a.m.

While she waited for Dr. Samuel Kajubi, Rebecca woke up the children and told them that their father was not well. By the time they came to his bedside, his breathing had slowed down to a death rattle. By the time Dr. Kajubi came, it was too late to do anything for him. Latimer breathed his last breath with the doctor right there at his bedside. She remembered him once saying, "God is amazing. A baby experiences pain while being born, but he cannot tell you about it. When your loved one is dying, you may ask them what you can do for them, but they cannot tell you." Within two months of each other, Rebecca had lost her beloved mother and the one and only love of her life: Latimer Kamya Musoke.

The emptiness in her belly turned into a bottomless pit that she wished she could crawl into. The world wasn't making sense anymore. How could God allow her to lose her mother and then a short two months later, her husband? They had done everything together, including taking care of mother. She had consulted him on every major decision she ever made in her adult life; but he had also taught her to stand on her own two feet. She had watched adoringly as he climbed the ladder of success and made her proud. She had been there to nurse him back to health after every illness. She had stayed by his side through prosperous times and times of lack, war times and peaceful times. How was she ever going to fulfil his dream of educating the children he loved so much? What about their dream of retiring on the farm together?

It was Monday morning, the 8th of October, 1979. Dr. Kajubi placed a death announcement on the radio at 6:00 a.m. Rebecca and her daughter Philippa prepared and dressed Latimer's body. Being a doctor must have helped Philippa handle the situation because Damallie would not come near the body. The house was already full of friends and relatives who had come to celebrate Damallie's graduation from the university. The celebration turned into mourning as the cooks realised that the food they were preparing was going to be for the wake instead. Two of the children were still in their university halls. Louise was brought home by her friends, unaware of her father's death until she arrived. Wilfred was fetched from his hall by the household help and informed while they were walking home. Rebecca looked into her precious children's faces and said, "Baana bange, mulabye!" ("Oh, my poor children!") but they instead tried to comfort her. The children had all spent time with their father over the weekend: the family had been together because of their grandmother's last funeral rites and the impending graduation and Independence holiday. She called them into the bedroom to say goodbye to their father for the last time. She remembered the words she had said to Latimer a few hours before and prayed that prayer again: "God, please give me that widow's purse."

Her brother-in-law suggested that they move the lumbe (wake) to his home in Lungujja. The university campus was going to be teeming with visitors who had come to attend the graduation ceremonies. Agnes and her husband, a doctor, offered to arrange for an autopsy at the hospital, then transport of the body to Lungujja. As her relatives and friends began to take over the logistics of the funeral arrangements, Rebecca felt the tension easing. But she could not afford to let herself grieve; not yet. As each of Latimer's relatives arrived at the lumbe, there was a fresh round of wailing. Yunia's arrival was especially poignant. No one could believe that Latimer had gone. They had all seen him or talked to him over the weekend. But they wanted to hear Rebecca's story over and over: how he had said goodbye, telling her what he would tell their mother when he saw her; how he had not only bought a graduation gown for Damallie, but also one for Louise who would be graduating the following year; how he had told the little ones they must do well in their exams because he wouldn't be there for them.

The lumbe lasted for two days. Rebecca didn't know how she got through it with the terrible headache she had. The pit in her belly had turned to a dull ache: a numbness that was, thankfully, muffling the brunt of the pain. She wasn't a wailer like many female mourners, but she had cried until there were no more tears to be shed; the coffers were empty. On Wednesday, Makerere University sent a coffin and a hearse to pick up Latimer's body for the funeral service at St. Francis Chapel, Makerere. The service was a blur, except for the faces of the numerous friends who came to pay their last respects to Latimer. Then it was time to take Latimer back to his home in Makonzi, Ssingo so that he could be buried next to his mother and father. Latimer's son, Henry, had arrived from America that morning. His sister had arranged his transport to Makonzi from the airport, but he missed it and arrived after the funeral was over. Latimer was buried at the feet of his beloved mother. Like Rebecca, she had only had two surviving sons and Latimer was the baby. She must have loved him as much or more than Rebecca did; and when the world could no longer cradle his genius, she had taken him home.

It was a year that had begun with fear, that turned to joy and hope for a brighter future. But it turned out to be the darkest year of Rebecca's life, as she struggled to come to terms with her losses. When she was growing up, her father had always been there for her to lean on, but after the death of her mother, he had become a shell of his former self and dependent on Rebecca. After she got married, she had looked to Latimer for leadership; now he had gone and she was the one who the children would be looking to. She had to be strong for them. Even though she didn't know it at the time, Latimer had not gone without thanking her and saying goodbye. She was there with him when he died and got to lovingly feed him and bathe him before he went. Her world seemed to be crumbling around her, but something deep inside kept reminding her of who she was and giving her the strength to look up. Rebecca had two sayings she always told the children: "God makes the back for the burden" and in Luganda: "Enjovu telemererwa masangagayo" (an elephant never fails to lift its own tusks). She would look to God for wisdom and strength.

Chapter Nineteen

Transitions

The family came home with many mourners still in tow. They spent one night at Lungujja, then returned to the house at Makerere. Patrick arrived several days after his father's funeral and his siblings drove him up to his father's gravesite. But as the weeks went by, life returned to normal for most of the mourners and they drifted away. Rebecca could feel the loneliness in every room of the house: in the bedroom where he had died in their bed; in the toilet, which she had last helped him to; in the dining room where they had sat at meals together for so many years; in the sitting room where they had entertained their guests together; on the stairs outside where he had once tripped and fallen. Sometimes she could see him and hear him talking to her. She would start to reply; then realise he wasn't really there. She kept saying to herself, "I have just lost my mother; how could I lose my husband, too?" Then she would tell herself, "Latimer has really gone forever; you need to be strong." She would later describe the pain as like biting into an unripe piece of fruit: no matter where you bite it, it's sour. You're sad, and you wish he was there to help carry the burden. You're happy; then you remember that he's not there to share the joy with you.

Adam came home from England a few weeks after his father was buried. During the last funeral rites, he was named as his father's heir. Rebecca started packing their things to move out of the house. On the morning of January 7th, 1980, Rebecca dreamt that she was having tea with Latimer.

He asked her, "Why are you still in this government house?"

She answered, "I have nowhere to go right now. Our house is occupied by the farmhands."

He said to her, "Mama, you know the house was given to me, not you. You had better move out." When Rebecca woke up, she rang her husband's nephew, Paulo Kawalya, and told him to come to the house with his lorry. She needed to move her things out of the house that day. Paulo came as asked and they started loading her things. At exactly 10 a.m., a Makerere University estate officer showed up at the house with a second gentleman. He wanted to speak to her directly.

He said, "Ma'am, you need to be out of this house by 4 p.m. This gentleman is moving in."

"Today?" she asked.

"Yes, ma'am," was the nondescript answer.

Rebecca knew now why Latimer had told her to get out of the house in her dream. She asked the estate officer for nothing more than a few extra hands to load her belongings into Paulo's lorry. Her in-laws had suggested that she evict the tenant from their rental house in Ntinda and move in there herself. As a widow with nothing but the income from the farm, she decided it was better to keep the tenant and keep getting the income. Over the twelve years in which they had lived on the university campus they had accumulated so much. Where were they going to store it all? They distributed her belongings to three different locations: some to her father's house in Mengo where the children were going to stay; some to her father's house in Mulawa where she was going to stay and some to a storeroom on the farm. Her father had told Rebecca she could have the house at Mengo, but Rebecca said 'no'. She would stay at Mulawa so that she could be close to the farm while she built her own house. Damallie and the younger children would stay at the Mengo house until then, and cousin Apollo Sendaula would give them a ride to work. Louise, Philippa and Wilfred were still at the university and would stay on in their halls.

The first thing Rebecca did was to send her father on to Mombasa as they had planned before Latimer passed away. He returned a few months later with his arm in a cast. Apparently, he had been knocked down by a scooter when he was crossing a street in Mombasa. He was on his way to visit a friend. The doctors had placed a plaster cast on the arm, but it wasn't healing properly. It was so painful to watch him try to feed himself with both a broken arm and broken teeth. Rebecca had the cast removed and he started physiotherapy. She then sent him on to England, where younger sister Damallie had asked if she could take care of him for a while.

It wasn't easy for Rebecca being so far away from the children, so she would spend many weekends at Mengo. One day, she returned to Mulawa and found that the room where she had stored her belongings had been broken into and the books and clothes torn and strewn around. It looked like an inside job. Rebecca wept. She looked for Latimer's M.B.E. medal and her heart sank when she found the empty box. As she continued searching, she found the medal under a pile of books. She thanked God. It might not have meant anything to the intruder, but to her, it was a precious memory of Latimer's best days.

Although nothing in her earlier life had prepared her for homelessness, Rebecca did not give in to despair. She still had her children and her widowed father to take care of; she still had to work on the farm and produce enough for them to live on. Thankfully, she still had her health and her strength, and she had the Toyota estate car she and Latimer had bought together. Then one day she got a letter from the bank informing her that her loan was in delinquency and in danger of default. They were threatening to repossess the farm! Rebecca fell to her knees and cried out to God. How could they take away her livelihood just like that? Rebecca drove to the bank at the earliest opportunity. Her bankers knew her well and were sympathetic when she outlined her plan to pay off the loan. Rebecca left the bank with their assurance and with determination in her heart that with God's help, she would pay off that loan.

Rebecca lost so many cows on the farm the year that Latimer died. It was as though the cows knew that their master had gone. She used the money she had received during the lumbe (*mabugo*) to build a little three-room cottage on the farm. It had a sitting room, two bedrooms and a small bathroom and storeroom on the side. Rebecca was so proud of her little house, the first one she ever built on her own. The children all came over to stay with her on the first night. They named the house 'Basoka kwavula' which means, 'You have to crawl before you can walk'. When all the other children went back to school, eldest daughter Damallie would come and spend weekends with her. The rest of the children and her former neighbour, Agnes, would also come over on some weekends. Agnes Sekabunga became a true friend in her time of need.

Becky and Bessie both passed their examinations and moved on to senior five and Makerere University respectively. The political situation remained unstable that year. No one believed that the elections held at the end of the year were truly free and fair; especially when they restored Milton Obote back to the presidency. His political rivals immediately started plotting his overthrow. And so began the most uncertain period in the history of the nation. There were increasing reports of guerrilla warfare all around the country. As a result, the military had roadblocks on all major thoroughfares. You never knew what they would take from you at the next roadblock. It was no longer safe to be on the road after dark. It wasn't safe to turn on the lights in your own house at night, either. Life became a chess game, with the winning move simply being able to stay alive.

One day, Rebecca's brother Joe was driving from Namugongo in a friend's car when he was stopped by government soldiers. Someone came to give Rebecca the bad news: your brother has been arrested. Her heart sank. Gentle, unassuming Joe; how could he survive in those conditions? No one could tell her where he had been taken to. Rebecca drove from prison to prison searching for her brother. Finally, she came to Makindye military barracks. She begged the head of the barracks to tell her if her brother was there.

He said, "Oh yes, there is a prisoner here who resembles you. He must be your brother. We can take you to see him."

She replied, "No sir, I don't need to see him right now; but please allow me to bring him some food regularly."

Rebecca thought if she had seen her brother right then, they would both simply have cried. Everyone had heard of the many atrocities that took place in that 'prison'. The prison wardens did allow her to start bringing him food. Rebecca would hide antibiotics and aspirin in the food she took him. The first time she saw Joe, she barely recognised him. He had lost so much weight, his right ear had been twisted out of shape and he was holding his right arm as if in pain, too. She did not cry, though, or do anything that would arouse the suspicion of the prison guards and make things worse for him.

Aunt Alex Nabatanzi insisted that she be the one to take him food regularly after that. She told Rebecca, "You're young and something could happen to you. I am old; it's better if I go." Her aunt would dress up in ragged clothes and Rebecca would drive her to the barracks. Whenever she arrived, she was required to taste the food herself before it could be given to the prisoner.

Rebecca was determined to do whatever she could to get her brother freed. Mr. and Mrs. Abraham Waligo had lived with

Latimer and Rebecca for a while when they were in England. It was they who had carried baby Elizabeth back to her grandmother. He and his wife and Latimer and Rebecca had remained friends throughout the years. Once when Latimer and Rebecca visited him on his farm, Latimer had admired his house and remarked that he had not been able to build a house for Rebecca. He referred to her as his 'Minister of Home Affairs' because she took care of all his needs. Mr. Waligo laughed. He said, "I will not be the one to build her a house either, but if there's anything else she ever needs, I'm your man." He was now a minister in the Uganda government. Rebecca went to him to see if he could help her figure out why her brother had been imprisoned.

Mr. Waligo soon came back to her with an answer. The report was that Joe had been arrested on suspicion of being a guerrilla because he had the same last name as his younger brother, Arnold, who had been a minister in the short-lived government of Professor Lule. Mr. Waligo was able to correct the mistaken identity and they agreed to let Joe go. Rebecca was overjoyed. She took Joe home to stay with her for a while. They were both there when the soldiers came to the house the first time. They demanded everyone's identity cards. Joe, who had just been released from prison, didn't have one. He must be a guerrilla, they said. Rebecca begged the soldiers not to arrest her brother again. She offered them anything they wanted. They took their watches and then demanded the car. Thankfully, they didn't get far.

Adam sent his mother a new Peugeot pick-up car from England that year. He wanted her to be able to supplement the income from the farm. The whole family waited with anticipation when it arrived in Mombasa. One day, there it was: a brand new royal blue car with shiny new tyres. Rebecca thought the safest place for it would be at Mulawa where her brother Dolphe was living. Within days, they had stolen three of the four tyres off the car. Rebecca thought the best thing to do then was to get the car on the road. She bought new tyres and had the pick-up built up into a matatu (taxi). She employed a driver for the taxi and sent him out to start making some money. The money did start rolling in... for three weeks!

Like Job's servants, someone came running back, one day, to tell her that the car had been stolen at gunpoint less than two kilometres from home. Rebecca jumped into her Toyota with the farm manager and they raced down the road. She stopped at the police station to get a police escort as she followed the trail of her car, her heart pounding. They drove through Kireka, Seeta, Mukono, Mpererwe and finally lost the trail near Kawempe. On the way, her own car got a flat tyre and they had to stop and fix it. They lost valuable time. The police continued their search and finally came up with a suspect, but the driver couldn't positively identify him. They had to let him go; and Rebecca had to let go of her dream car.

It was a day like any other that December in 1980. The sun was shining, the bees were buzzing and the Agama lizards were lying lazily on the rocks. Everyone else was bustling on with life, seemingly indifferent to her plight. How was she going to tell Adam that the car he had just sent, and probably still owed thousands of pounds on, was lost? How much money could she get on her insurance claim in these uncertain times? And whom could she talk to about it? Latimer and mother were gone. Her father was far away in England. That was without a doubt a low point.

On New Year's Eve, 1981, the children were home to celebrate the new year with her. But what kind of new year would it be? Rebecca could not hold back the tears when she paused to think of something to be thankful for. There appeared to be only the faintest glimmer of light on the horizon of hope. The country she and Latimer had returned to twenty years earlier had been full of hope for a bright future for them and all the ensuing generations. Now it was spiralling downward into an abyss of terror. What would the future hold for those generations? But the children encouraged Rebecca that all was not lost: they still had each other; they had food to eat and clothes on their backs; they were all still in school and doing well in their studies; God would take care of them, as she herself had always reminded them.

Chapter Twenty

Perilous Times

In the midst of all the discouraging news, there *were* moments of unspeakable joy. Earlier that year, Louise had graduated from Makerere University School of Medicine at the top of her class! Rebecca shed tears of joy at the news, but was sad that Latimer was not there to share that moment. He had worked so hard for it; they had both prayed with trepidation when she almost didn't take her A-level examinations. She was rewarded with an internship at Nsambya Hospital. The year after that, Philippa also graduated from medical school near the top of her class! A year later, Wilfred graduated as a civil engineer. She had three engineers and two doctors so far in the family. Rebecca could only say to God, "Mukama, Gwe mubeezi wange; n'ensobola okusomesa abaana? Ekitiibwa kidde gyoli!" (Lord, You are my helper; how did I manage to educate those children? To You alone be the glory!")

Rebecca was also grateful that Latimer's brother, Cranimer Kabali, and his family stepped in and became her children's father and brothers. The Kabali's residence in Lungujja became the site of all the graduation parties and engagement ceremonies. When eldest daughter Damallie was going to get married, she knew times were hard and told her mother she would rent a wedding dress. Her cousin Paulo stepped in. He said, "No way! Musoke would turn over in his grave! I will pay for the wedding dress and the 'changing' dress and the bridesmaids' dresses." Cousin Louise Sserunjogi found a tailor and the whole family chipped in and gave Damallie a beautiful wedding. The children's grandfather was still away in London, so Rebecca invited Uncle Christopher Sekuuma and his wife to sit at the family's high table. A year later, when daughter Philippa was getting married, the extended family were there to support her too. At her wedding reception, Philippa gave a speech in which she thanked her mother for being there for them all, despite everything she had been through since they had lost their father. Rebecca couldn't keep back the tears. She cried at each of her children's weddings, thinking of how much she would have loved to have Latimer at her side and how proud he would have been.

Rebecca's father came home from England in 1982. His teeth had been operated on and were perfect, and with appropriate physiotherapy, his arm had healed. He could now feed himself and even write again, something he loved to do. He found her still living in her little house 'Basoka kwavula'. She asked him to move in with her so that she could take care of him. Even with all the turmoil, there was a cosy feeling to having him nearby. It almost reminded her of the 'good old days' when she and her father would take long walks together and discuss her plans for the future. He often walked alone now; down the grassy driveway to the main road. There he would cross the road, walk several yards down the road and turn right towards the family graveyard. He would sit for hours at mother's graveside. She hoped, rather than saw that it gave him comfort and the will to go on living.

These were not easy times. The area around Namugongo had become known as a guerrilla stronghold. The alarm would sound suddenly as soldiers poured out into the surrounding area. People would decamp immediately, leaving their homes with nothing more than the clothes on their backs. Rebecca would gather her photo albums, put her father in the car and they would drive off to her daughter Louise's house in Kitante Courts. Twice, the soldiers came to her little house on the farm, demanding money, while she and her father were there. Rebecca gave them the little she had. When they were not satisfied, they beat her and kicked her, demanding more. A boy who appeared to be no more than 14 years old was hitting her with the butt of his gun. She said to him, "Young man, how can you beat me? You are younger than all my children." Outside, they demanded the keys of her car. She gave them up readily. The first time, they only got as far as the main road. It wasn't advisable to keep much petrol in your car. Someone came running to tell her that her car had been abandoned not far away.

The next time they came, they tried to take Rebecca's radiogram from her sitting room. In a stroke of genius, Rebecca quickly severed the wires in the back and then showed the soldiers that it was broken. Then they tried to take the car, but the young soldier sitting in the driver's seat must not have ever taken driving lessons. He put the car in reverse and almost hit the wall; he put it in first gear and promptly crashed into her brother Myers' tractor that was parked in the driveway.

Another soldier who was watching asked Rebecca, "Where is your husband?"

She replied, "I am a widow."

He turned to the young soldier who was still trying to get the car moving and said, "Get out of the car! This lady is a widow. That's bad luck!" They left her car sitting in the driveway. Rebecca had named her car 'Muddu awulira' (obedient servant) because it had served her faithfully for so many years. It didn't let her down now!

One of Rebecca's part-time farm hands, Kasiita, earned her eternal gratitude during these perilous times. He and Peter, another local with whom he regularly drank alcohol, were in hiding during patrol operations by government soldiers around the farm. Out the two men came: "Owaye, owaye, ebisajja bigenze," ("Hey, hey, they've gone") one of them said within earshot of the soldiers. The soldiers proceeded to beat and hack them. Peter received a deep cut on the head and Kasiita one on the leg. Somehow their lives were spared. As the village gradually came out of hiding (Rebecca herself never took cover in the bushes), the two were found in very poor shape. She braved the roadblocks and interrogations to take them to hospital for stitching. In those days, anybody appearing at a hospital with wounds was suspected to be a bandit. She implored the nurses and doctors to help her workers who had fallen amongst 'thieves'. Peter remained with a deep scar on his forehead and Kasiita one on his leg. Peter later passed away, but Kasiita remained in Rebecca's employ for decades, in gratitude, while still enjoying his daily drink.

Rebecca was thankful that the soldiers never beat her elderly father; and despite the beatings, she was never raped. She would not allow her daughters to come and stay at the farm in those days. Eldest daughter Damallie was now living in Nairobi with her husband, Isaac. One day, Rebecca heard a car pull up to the house. She opened the door to see Damallie standing there with a suitcase in hand. Rebecca stared at her in surprise and said, "What are you doing here?" She was nine months pregnant.

"Mummy, I don't want to have my baby born in Kenya!" She moved in.

A few days later they heard an alarm. They opened the door to see people running and heard gunfire. The soldiers were coming! Rebecca grabbed her daughter's suitcase and bundled her father and daughter into her car. They drove to town where they spent the next several days. After three or four days, Rebecca returned to the farm. The cows were scattered and hungry because everyone had to decamp when the soldiers came, but everything seemed calm now. Thankfully, the cows had not been stolen or slaughtered by the soldiers. She could barely remember the days when she and Latimer had owned over one hundred head of cattle. She now had less than twenty-five. After a week, she fetched her father and daughter.

That night, Damallie told her mother she was feeling uncomfortable. Rebecca thought: 'Well, it's her first baby; she's probably not ready to deliver yet.' She went into the kitchen. A short while later she came back. She noticed that Damallie's baby had 'dropped'. Time to panic! She had had seven babies of her own, but she had never delivered someone else's baby. There was no driving to a hospital in the middle of the night in these perilous times. Rebecca went and fetched the local midwife. The midwife checked her daughter and told them she was ready to have the baby. She didn't have her delivery equipment with her, though. It was at her clinic in Kireka.

Rebecca asked her father to watch her daughter while she and the midwife drove off to pick up her equipment. She had never driven that three-kilometre stretch of road so fast in her life. Thankfully, since it was after midnight, there were no other cars on the road. When they returned, her father was standing outside. Rebecca asked him what had happened.

"I heard her screaming and thought, 'Oh my God, who is going to deliver this baby?' I came out to see what was taking you so long," he replied.

Rebecca and the midwife ran into the house and prepared the labouring mother for delivery. Rebecca was anxious that her daughter may not be able to deliver without the help of modern medical facilities in a hospital, but the midwife reassured her that everything was progressing normally. Rebecca's first grandchild was born right there on the floor of her bedroom in 'Basoka kwavula'. The irony of a doctor's grandchild being born outside a hospital wasn't lost on Rebecca, but as Latimer used to say, "Anyone who says there is no God just needs to see a baby being born!"

Great grandfather heard the cries of the baby and gave a whoop of joy. Rebecca looked at her baby granddaughter and thanked the Lord who had once again performed a miracle for them. She looked so tiny though, maybe she was premature. They wrapped her warmly in blankets and put her under a bright light. In the morning, they drove mother and baby to Mulago Hospital where they found her other daughter, Philippa. Rebecca announced to her, "Surprise! The baby is already here!" Mother and baby were fine. They were admitted and discharged after only one day. Rebecca affectionately named her granddaughter 'Baby Kagabi' because of her clan. That little baby cried so much the first few weeks; maybe she knew something about the perilous times she had been born into. Thankfully, both grandmothers were there to help.

On leaving the hospital, they drove mother and baby Pauline to the house at Mengo. Because of the nearby military barracks there were soldiers all around. Nursing and changing the baby at night were candlelight affairs, as they still could not risk turning on the lights. Finally, after six weeks, Damallie was ready to return to Nairobi with her baby. Rebecca had her father in the car when they drove them to the airport. On the way, one of the tyres on the Toyota went flat. Rebecca changed the tyre herself and they drove another couple of kilometres before they realised the spare tyre had gone flat too. That's when Rebecca got out of the car and flagged down another car to get her daughter and granddaughter to the airport. Even if she couldn't see them off at the airport, Rebecca was relieved to see them go. With them in Nairobi, she had two less people to worry about.

In the early 1980s, a women's council was formed to help the women who had become widowed during the regime of Idi Amin. Rebecca was elected chairman of the East Mpigi Constituency (E.P.C.). She was able to get the widows loans at low interest rates; help them buy second-hand clothes for their children; assist them in buying food at the farmer's markets; and also help them start their own small businesses. Once she was driving from an E.P. C. meeting in Gayaza when she was flagged down by some soldiers. Rebecca turned on her indicator and slowed down. Just as she was about to pull up alongside them, she gunned the engine and took off down the road. She did not let her foot off the accelerator until she reached Komamboga and the junction that would have taken her to Mr. Waligo's house. As soon as she turned off the main road, Rebecca jumped out of her car and hid herself in one of the nearby shops. The soldiers arrived in their jeep, looked around for her and drove off when they couldn't see her. She waited for a little while, then got back into her car and drove home. After so many encounters with soldiers, she was fearless.

One day, Rebecca drove down to Mr. Cranimer Kabali's shop. The two of them had an appointment with a lawyer, but Cranimer wasn't there. When she asked the grandchildren where her brother-in-law was, they replied, "They picked him up." Rebecca knew exactly what that meant: he had been 'arrested' by government soldiers. She drove to his home and broke the news to his wife. The poor woman didn't want to believe it; hoping in her heart that it was just a rumour. Rebecca drove her sister-in-law back to the shop so that she could hear the account of his disappearance first-hand. This time, no amount of detective work could establish his whereabouts. They could not even find anyone who knew whether he had been killed or where his remains were. It was 1984. They had lost Yunia at the end of 1983 and now Cranimer had disappeared.

Several years later, a young man showed up at the shop asking if this was the shop that belonged to Mr. Kabali. Immediately, everyone gathered around to hear what the young man had to say. After he was seated, he told them that he and many others had been rounded up the same day that Mr. Kabali had been taken away. He remembered that Mr. Kabali annoyed the soldiers because every one of his statements was punctuated with a reference to the Kabaka. He had had a chance to speak to the distinguished-looking gentleman, who requested that if he didn't survive and the young man did, he would go to this very location and tell his family what had happened to him.

The young man had agreed but was doubtful if he would make it out alive either. They were being tortured every day. Before long, they were driven blindfolded on the back of a lorry to a location far away from Kampala. When they got to their destination, they were all herded off the lorry and then literally hacked to death. The young man described how he had received a blow to the head, but he had survived by hiding under the dead bodies. When everything had been quiet for a while, he called out. He heard one voice in response. Another young man was alive, barely; he could see that he had lost a lot of blood. They were in a deserted, bushy patch of land with no sign of civilisation. He promised the other young man that he would return with some water as soon as he could. When he returned, the other man was dead.

The young man told them that he had been rescued by the guerrillas and been forced to join them. Now that there was a new regime in power, he had come to show them the field where their father had been killed. Like everyone else on that lorry, he had been killed by a blow to the head. Maybe they would be able to recognise his remains.

Rebecca didn't hesitate to gather her brother-in-law's family and they drove out to the field directed by the young man. They started digging, not knowing what to expect. Rebecca had never seen a field with so many skulls in her life before. She was the one who found her brother-in-law's skull. She recognised where the gap had been between his teeth and sure enough, there was the blow to the skull. Mrs. Kabali fainted at the site of her husband's remains; she recognised the shirt he had been wearing the day he disappeared. They managed to revive her with some tea, then they wrapped up the skull and a few bones and headed home.

Rebecca washed off the skull and wrapped it again in preparation for the lumbe (wake). The family had gathered to mourn their father and brother, but some were not sure it was really him. Someone said, "If it's really him, let him show us a sign." There was a strip light in the dining room that had not worked for a long time. It suddenly lit up. Everyone decided that it was a sign from Mr. Kabali and were grateful for it. The next day, they took his remains to Makonzi, Ssingo and buried him next to his parents and his younger brother, Latimer.

Rebecca (back row, 2nd left) with her extended family at Mulawa. 1969

Rebecca with her husband and children. 1978

Rebecca with her father, her sister, her
children and son-in-law Kasana. 1983

Rebecca with her brothers and sister in her cottage.

Rebecca with the Lwai-Lumes in Nairobi and
grandchildren Igeme, Muwanse and Mbakire.

Rebecca with her daughter-in-law and grandchildren
in London: Gibwa and Kabali Musoke.

Rebecca with her children, grandchildren and in-laws at her 70th birthday celebration. 2002

Rebecca with Damallie, Philippa, the Kaggwas
and grandchildren: Cathy, Liza and Daudi.

Rebecca with her sister and three oldest
grandchildren: Philip, Pauline and Jeremiah.

Rebecca attending National Service

Rebecca with her cows on Nabwojjo Farm

Chapter Twenty-One

Letting Go

Rebecca's father was still living with her in her little cottage. During this time, Rebecca assisted him in administering his estate with his advisor, Mr. Munyigwa. There were so many land issues to resolve. Many friends would come by the house to visit him as well. He had missed that while he was in England. One of them was his good friend, Cardinal Emmanuel Nsubuga, who always referred to Rebecca's father as his Kojja (maternal uncle). He had donated the bricks Rebecca was using to build a new house on the farm. Years ago, she and Latimer had had a brick maker build bricks for their rental houses in Ntinda and Jinja in the compound of their house at Nakasero. They discovered there were restrictions on such activity on government property when they were taken to court and had to pay a fine. Here, there were no restrictions on what Rebecca could do.

She built her new house around the one that she and Latimer had built thirty years earlier because it was situated at the very summit of the hill. She replanted her plantain and vegetable garden and felt settled; as if she was home. From her front veranda, she could look out over the surrounding landscape in every direction and see the top of the Namugongo Catholic Martyr's Shrine. Just as she and Latimer had envisioned, she was surrounded by her domestic animals: a cat, dogs, chickens, turkeys, cows and goats. She even had a tame monkey once. When the cows were in the upper paddocks, she could watch them grazing peacefully on the lush, green grass. Monkeys lurked in the surrounding trees, awaiting any opportunity to scamper down and grab a stray piece of fruit. A pair of Uganda cranes had adopted her farm as their home and could be seen doing their stately march around the paddocks like sentinels. At night, she could hear the howl of foxes and the laugh of hyenas. She saw a large python a couple of times; fortunately, it was at a distance.

Rebecca's new house was built with three bedrooms, including one for her father. But her father would never live to see the finished house. Bishop Ernest Shalita, another friend, invited him to visit him in Mbarara and he was happy to oblige. The two friends flew down there together. While he was there, Rebecca's father became gravely ill and had to be rushed back to Kampala by road. Rebecca tried in vain to bring him back by air, but the airlines were on strike. It was a harrowing 250-kilometre journey for an old, infirm gentleman to make. By the time he arrived in Kampala, her father was too weak to have the surgery he needed for benign prostatic hypertrophy (an enlarged prostate gland that was obstructing the emptying of the bladder). The toxins were slowly building up in his body, but he was not in severe pain.

He was admitted to hospital for palliative care. While he was there, his brother Christopher came to visit him. They were both old men in their 80s by now; each with a stoop and a full head of grey hair; still recognizable as brothers, although Kupliano was a head taller. Kupliano apologised to his brother for not getting up to greet him. Christopher responded similarly in jest: "Aleph, you were always the one on the move; it's time for you to keep still and let me do the moving." They laughed quietly. His brother had referred to him by his childhood nickname. All that had happened in-between was forgiven and forgotten.

Rebecca took care of her beloved father in his final days, just as she had taken care of her mother. She regretted letting him go to Mbarara, but she made sure that he got the very best of nursing care at Namirembe Hospital. She had been so close to her father. All her life she had been 'Daddy's little girl'; but when the time came, she was ready to let him go. He had survived his beloved Damali for six long years, some of them very painful years. He had been with Rebecca through the darkest days of her life and now he needed to rest. His faith in God had never wavered and she knew his prayers had sustained them both, as well as all his children and grandchildren. She was at his bedside when he said to her, "Ba Damali bampita," and breathed his last breath here on earth. She knew exactly whom he was talking about: his mother and his wife, both of whom had been named Damali, were calling him home.

He died on June 6th, 1985, almost a year to the day after he had been present for the birth of his great grandchild, the 'Little Kagabi'. They laid him to rest next to his beloved Damali. Rebecca's brother, Joe, was named his father's heir, but he had chosen Rebecca, together with his friend Mr. Kaddu, to be the executors of his estate. This did not go down well with some members of the family and was to cause Rebecca much pain in the future. To make matters worse, Mr. Kaddu died soon after their father, so Rebecca was left as the sole executor of her father's estate.

Most of Rebecca's children had left home by now. The political situation was still uncertain and only three of her children were able to attend the funeral of their grandfather. Adam had been the first to leave in 1972. The next one to leave was Bessie. She left for America in 1981. In 1982, daughter Damallie and her husband went to England. They returned in 1983, but then moved to Nairobi when her husband got a job there. Louise left for England in 1983 and was there until she completed her studies and came back to get married in 1986. Philippa and her husband went to America at the beginning of 1985, soon after their son was born. Becky moved to Nairobi when she finished her university degree in 1985, too. Maybe they had all inherited that travel bug that their grandfather had.

Rebecca travelled to Nairobi with Becky that year. She remembered very well the journeys to Nairobi with her father by train in the 1950s. But it wasn't time to reminisce over bygone days. There was no longer a train by which you could travel from Kampala to Nairobi, so they had to take a bus. The bus she and Becky were travelling in was involved in an accident, but thankfully, they arrived unharmed. Damallie was about to have her second baby and this time, Rebecca wasn't going to let her come to Kampala. Bessie was visiting from America, but she wouldn't let her travel to Uganda, either. The situation was too volatile. Milton Obote's government had been overthrown by Tito Okello, the fourth change of government since the overthrow of Idi Amin. Tito Okello's government was under threat from the guerrilla war that had been mounted by Yoweri Museveni. Rebecca saw her third grandchild, Philip, delivered safely at Mater Misericordiae Hospital in Nairobi.

She was still over there helping her daughter with the newborn when Pauline, the 'Little Kagabi', became ill. She was diagnosed with a viral infection. Her mother was still nursing the baby, so she wasn't allowed to visit her in hospital. It fell to Rebecca to watch over her first grandchild. They couldn't afford a private room at Gertrude's Garden Children's Hospital, so a neighbour would drive Rebecca to the hospital in the morning and pick her up in the evening. She was there every day, even outside visiting hours, until she nursed her 'Little Kagabi' back to health.

That wasn't the last time Rebecca acted as 'guardian angel' over a grandchild. Baby Philip had to have corrective plaster casts placed on his legs, so his parents decided to leave both children with their grandmother in Kampala until the next doctor's review. The baby was nine months old when he developed pneumonia. He was admitted to Old Mulago Hospital. Damallie and her husband, Isaac, came rushing back from Nairobi. After a couple of days, the baby developed a rash. He was diagnosed with measles and transferred to the measles ward. He was still on oxygen and had to share a bed with other children who were dependent on oxygen. At least four of the other children he shared oxygen with during that hospitalisation did not make it.

Her daughter later recounted:

> "Mum was a tower of strength not only to me but to all the mothers in the ward. The medical staff would leave at 6:00 p.m. They would give out whatever medication was required for the night and then we were on our own. If there was an emergency at night, the mothers would call Mum. They thought she had some medical training because the nurses would tell her what to do if anyone needed help. One night the oxygen ran out, so she went looking for oxygen in the other wards. She came back with a cylinder. Another night a child was dying. She went to the women's ward and came back with a nurse."

One day, Professor Christopher Ndugwa came to the ward. Professor Ndugwa was a paediatrician who had worked with Latimer. He had taken over as head of the department after Latimer's death. He recognised Rebecca and asked her what she was doing there. Rebecca was only too happy to have him examine her grandson. After his examination, he instructed the medical staff to have the baby checked for malaria. Within hours of being properly diagnosed and starting treatment,

Philip was recovering. The rash that had been misdiagnosed as measles was simply a reaction to the penicillin he was being given for 'pneumonia'. They were all so thankful to God and grateful to Professor Ndugwa for coming in the nick of time. His answer was philosophical: "How could we let Professor Latimer Musoke's grandchild die of malaria? He single-handedly carried the acute care children's ward at Mulago Hospital through its darkest days."

While Rebecca was in Nairobi, Uncle Christopher became ill. His wife and the rest of the family wanted Rebecca to come home and be his caretaker. Everyone knew how well she had cared for her own mother and father while they were ill and in hospital. There was one thing Rebecca had never allowed her parents to develop while hospitalised: a bedsore. She was saddened to discover her uncle on his deathbed by the time she returned to Kampala. He passed away that December, on Christmas day, and was buried in the family graveyard at Kyaliwajjala.

Sometimes it was lonely for Rebecca, with her parents and her husband gone and her sister and all the children scattered around the world. She would remember with nostalgia the days when their home was full of children and it was rare to get a quiet moment. She wasn't much of a reader, nor did she enjoy watching television. At the end of each day, she would complete the ledger for the farm in her diary and write down whatever else she thought was worth noting; then she would listen to the radio as she knitted. For many years, whenever she was in trouble, she would dream of Latimer coming to her and saying, "Ng'olabye. Kankufumbire chai onywe." ("What a pity. Let me bring you some tea"). Then he would bring the chai and they would drink it together. She would wake up hearing his voice encouraging her to be strong. He always used to say, "Don't cry over spilt milk!"

One day, Rebecca gathered up the courage to listen to some of Latimer's favourite classical music on his eight-track tapes. To her surprise, she suddenly heard his voice introducing the next piece of music. His voice was as clear and vivid as if he was in the room with her. On one tape, she heard him giving a medical lecture on the treatment of food poisoning. Rebecca couldn't believe what a treasure she had found; and it had taken her seven years to discover it! She had come to terms with the untimely death of her husband, but hearing his voice again brought the tears on. She remembered a famous quote she had read once: *"Our cause was never more in danger than at such a time – when one of God's creatures left desolate, seemingly abandoned, by sheer will power continues to obey."* [5]

She was eloquently quoting C.S. Lewis, but Rebecca still had to tell herself, "God has an assignment for each one of us. Latimer's duty was finished. Mine still has to go on, so I will keep on struggling. I thank God for the blessings He has given me. My health has been good and He is still keeping me well. God somehow houses His presence in empty houses. When I come back to the house alone, a house that should have been home to two of us, I feel God's presence here. I pray for other people like me who come back to empty houses, that their houses will be housed by God's presence."

Chapter Twenty-Two

Renaissance

By January 1986 when President Yoweri Museveni finally ousted Tito Okello's government and took over the presidency, Uganda was tired of all the wars. The people were ready for peace and hoped the new president would have the will and the means to bring it about. His National Resistance Movement (N.R.M.) established resistance councils to govern at the local level, which eventually became local councils. During Idi Amin's government, all mailo land (land privately owned in Buganda) had been converted to 99 year leases. Museveni's government reinstated mailo land, but also introduced a law that any squatter who had been in a place for more than 12 years was a bona fide squatter and could not be evicted. They *were* required to pay 'busulu' (taxes) to the landowners.

Rebecca was elected to her local council (L.C.) as the treasurer. The chairperson was Mrs. Alice Sekagya and they quickly became good friends. The council had many responsibilities but very little money with which to carry out their duties. They were only allowed to levy 1000 shillings from anyone who petitioned for a license. Many community projects that were started by the council could not be finished, so Rebecca would chip in and make up the difference. One of these projects involved construction around an underground wellspring that was used by the whole village as a water supply. The children would often step in it and muddy the water while trying to fill their jerry cans. Rebecca had a wall built around it and the water siphoned through a pipe so that they no longer had to step in it. She was able to provide clean water for all those who needed it.

Until she was elected to the L.C., Rebecca had thought she knew her neighbours pretty well. The villagers brought endless grievances to the council and they often took bribes and betrayed one another. They particularly disliked landowners like her. Sometimes, the neighbours would dig up the poles in her paddock fences and use them for firewood and the barbed wire would collapse. Then her cows would breach the fences and 'raid' the vegetable gardens of neighbouring squatters. It was almost with glee that they showed up to claim their compensation. When national service 'muchaka, muchaka' was recommended for the general population, Rebecca volunteered. Everyone was surprised that, at her age, Rebecca joined in wholeheartedly and finished the course without missing a single class. She took the opportunity to demystify the gun by learning to fire one herself. Not that Rebecca was afraid for her life anymore; it was just the challenge of it.

It was like coming out of the dark ages into the Renaissance! The political, economic and social climate of Uganda was slowly improving under President Yoweri Museveni. That year, Rebecca's daughter, Louise, was coming home from England to get married to Nabeta. Rebecca's sister, Damallie, would be coming home from England for a visit shortly after that. She hadn't seen her sister since they had buried their father together a year earlier. Over the years, they had become not only true sisters but the best of friends; sharing secrets like she had shared with her father, long after he had gone. Rebecca had worked hard to educate her children and God had kept his promise to her and given her that widow's purse. Becky had managed to finish her bachelor's degree in commerce at Makerere University and subsequently, her professional course in accounting. The only one she was worried about was Bessie in America. She had been accepted to several top schools, including Johns Hopkins University, but had been unable to find the funds to start medical school. Rebecca had left no stone unturned in trying to help her. They had written to numerous organisations, but two years had gone by with no progress in her career. That year, Latimer's life insurance policy finally matured and Rebecca was able to send Bessie the funds to start medical school at Emory University. It was amazing: even in death, Latimer was making sure his children achieved their dreams.

The following year, Rebecca was able to obtain foreign exchange from the bank. She sold some of her land and sent the money to Bessie to start her second year. Then President Museveni devalued the currency and all the money that Rebecca had saved became worthless. Foreign exchange was not available and Bessie had to drop out of medical school in her third year. It was painful for Rebecca, knowing that she had no avenue through which she could assist her daughter. She would never forget the day when she received a telegram from Bessie. It read, 'Praise the Lord, back in school!' Rebecca burst into tears of joy. She could not imagine by what miracle her daughter had managed to re-enrol in school. Her daughter wrote a letter explaining how: Not wanting her to fall behind, Bessie's classmates had collected the funds she needed together among themselves. They wanted to make sure she completed her third year with them and graduated on time. Rebecca could only fall on her knees and thank God for yet another unexpected blessing.

Now that her children were all established in their careers, there was nothing to stop Rebecca from enjoying the fruits of her labour. Her faith in God had been rewarded and her personal faith renewed. She had finally paid off the hefty loan that she and Latimer had taken out for the farm twenty years earlier and she had just won a major court battle. A year after Latimer passed away, someone posing as his son had illegally sold their property in Ntinda. The tenants came to ask Rebecca why she was evicting them. She knew that she hadn't served them an eviction order. That's when she found out that the imposter had taken their land titles out of the bank where Latimer had left them. The property had been sold twice. She had no other recourse than to fight the case in court. The registered 'owners' were in possession of stolen property. Rebecca spent the next five years fighting for her house in Ntinda, followed by several years battling for Latimer's land in Katwe, which the imposter had also sold.

Rebecca had a lawyer, but she did a lot of the investigative legwork herself and testified on her own behalf. After a two year-long court battle, judgement was passed in her favour. The verdict was appealed and the case dragged on for another two years. At the end of it all, the appeal was dismissed. She had finally won the case. It had taken a lot of guts, sweat and tears, but she had her property back. On more than one occasion, Rebecca had considered giving up the fight, but she said to herself, "I built that house with my own hands, I cannot give it up." She had known her rights. But she acknowledged the God who had given her the strength to keep on fighting month after month, year after year. 'David Sejjaaka Nalima versus Rebecca Musoke' (Civil Appeal No. 12 of 1985) remains a landmark case in the legal system of Uganda. Many years later when her granddaughter, Pauline, was in law school, she told her grandmother, "Jjajja we studied about your case in class today."

The children and her sister encouraged Rebecca to take a break, so she handed over the daily running of the farm to a relative and boarded a plane for England for the first time since she and Latimer had returned in 1962. It was exactly 25 years later. She was looking forward to seeing how much the rest of the world had changed. The journey was much shorter than the first one she remembered in 1952 or the second one in 1960. There were no stops along the way from Entebbe to London. This time she was alone; but her sister, Damallie, was there waiting for her. She was going to make sure her sister had a wonderful time. And she did!

Damallie was away at school teaching all day, but Rebecca wasn't lonely. She loved to hop on the bus, then catch the tube to all the interesting shops she had discovered. She loved to walk in the neighbourhood and make friends among the people she met. She loved to go sightseeing and visit famous museums and churches. Sometimes alone, sometimes with Damallie or her friend Kit, she would rediscover all the places she used to visit a lifetime ago. She even went to Hampstead and saw the house where they had lived when Elizabeth was a baby. She would look up relatives and old friends like Dr. Shannon (a Veterinarian) and Dr. Stanfield (a Paediatrician) who had worked with them in Uganda when Latimer was still alive. The families had all become good friends. Eldest son Adam still lived in England and was married to Florence now. He was there to ferry Rebecca around when he wasn't at work. Crown Prince Ronald Mutebi was there, too, and she liked to think their meeting had something to do with him choosing to move back to Uganda in 1988. Perhaps now that the new regime was firmly established, his kingdom would finally be restored.

On her next trip to London, Rebecca boarded the plane for her first trip to America. Philippa was finishing her postgraduate studies in Paediatrics and Bessie was finishing medical school. She was excited because she was going to visit a place she had never been to before. She arrived in America in the middle of summer, 1989. It was hotter in Kentucky and Georgia than she had imagined it could be in this temperate region of the world. Everything seemed so big! It didn't seem like the petrol crisis had ever reached this part of the world.

The people, the houses, the cars and the roads were all larger-than-life. And all so clean. Why were their houses shaped like oversize matchboxes? And everything opposite to the way it was done in England? The people were very friendly, but they had a quaint habit of speaking through their noses. Maybe that's what caused their funny accents.

Rebecca had always enjoyed experiencing new things and meeting new people. They took a long drive across several Eastern states and she got to see the countryside. Just as she had done in London, she took long walks, exploring the neighbourhoods where her daughters lived. She made friends wherever she went. One night when Philippa was on call, she came home to find that Rebecca had spent the whole night up talking to her friend, Robinah. Rebecca got to spend time with her eldest grandson, Jeremiah, whom she had only seen once after his parents left Uganda when he was only three weeks old. He was old enough now to disappear on his own and make his mother and grandmother frantic; until they found him at a neighbour's house eating pizza. Rebecca also got to meet Bessie's American classmates, Tami Fisk and Helen Roberts, who had been instrumental in helping her get back into medical school. She wrote a personal note of thanks to each of their parents. Rebecca never forgot the lessons her mother taught her: be grateful, and remember the good that others do to you.

Although her children were scattered around the world just like she and her siblings had once been, Rebecca wasn't going to miss out on seeing her grandchildren grow up. Two new grandchildren were born in England: Gibwa and Kabali, two in Nairobi: Igeme and Muwanse and one in Kampala: Liza. Rebecca made sure she did not miss the birth of Louise's firstborn Igeme, her fourth grandchild, who was born in early 1988. She spent two months in Nairobi helping her daughter. She didn't miss the birth of her next grandchild, Muwanse, two years later, either. While she was there, Rebecca would get up early and make her way downstairs. She crept downstairs carefully and even knew which step creaked, so as not to step on it. She prepared endless flasks of millet porridge for her daughter, which ensured plenty of milk for the baby. This time she could only spend one month with Louise, though, because Becky was getting married in Kampala, and preparations for the engagement ceremonies between Fred and Becky were about to begin.

Chapter Twenty-Three

Restoration

A new age was dawning and Rebecca was grateful to be alive to see it. The Soviet empire was crumbling, Germany was reunified and Nelson Mandela was set free from prison after twenty-seven years! Peace and prosperity were thriving in Uganda; but so was the epidemic of HIV and AIDS. No one could tell where this disease had come from and whether there would ever be a cure. As soon as you saw someone losing weight unexpectedly, you knew that they were not long for this world. All around her, children were being orphaned and mothers and fathers were losing their children. Funerals became as commonplace as weddings. President Museveni took the bold step of acknowledging the severity of the epidemic to the world, and aggressively campaigning against the behaviours that were spreading the disease. Sadly, its prevalence appeared to run parallel with the very culture of polygamy that was ubiquitous in the nation.

Richard Walugembe, the crown prince's younger brother, fell ill. His aunts in England took care of him for six months until it was clear that his illness was terminal. He was very weak when he returned to Uganda in 1992, but his good sense of humour was still intact. Rebecca had always been close to him and she visited him regularly during his illness, taking her grandchildren along to amuse him. He asked to visit her farm and she took him there for a day's outing. He loved it. When he passed away, Rebecca attended the funeral service, but, like the crown prince, she was not permitted to attend the interment at Kasubi Nabulagala. She returned to the palace at Banda where numerous mourners had gathered to express their condolences to Crown Prince Ronald Muwenda Mutebi and the rest of the family.

The resurrection of the Kingdom of Buganda began in stages the following year. First, the restoration of the Lubiri (palace) and Bulange (the parliament building) to the kingdom took place early that year. Next, preparations began for the coronation of the crown prince at Buddo on the 31st of July, 1993. It was an exciting time to be alive in Buganda and Rebecca was required to be present at each of the kingdom functions. There had been some question about who was the rightful Mugema (head of the Nkima clan who performs the coronation), but the crown prince had fulfilled all that protocol required and the preparations were on track. The Baganda have an ingenious method of equitable sharing in the reigning monarch's power over his subjects from generation to generation. Unlike commoners and other members of the royal family, once chosen, the crown prince takes on the clan of his mother, not his father. Since no one can marry within their own clan, every succeeding Kabaka hails from a different clan from that of his father; ensuring bragging rights to a different clan for at least a generation.

Rebecca spent the night before the coronation at the Banda Palace. A special meal was cooked for the prospective king, a taste of which Rebecca had to give him while he was sitting on her lap. She charged him with the task ahead of him with the words, "Okuze. Genda ofuge Obuganda!" ("You're a man now. Go and rule the Kingdom of Buganda!") The next morning, Rebecca and her brother Myers, (the Ssabaganzi, special uncle to the king in charge of security), were transported to the Naggalabi coronation site at Buddo. A car had been sent for them by soon-to-be-appointed Prime Minister, Joseph Mulwanyammuli Ssemwogerere. The occasion promised to be as resplendent and elaborate as that which she had witnessed as a little girl in 1942, but now, she could see it through the eyes of an adult. There were plenty of dignitaries and crowds of adoring subjects just as there had been fifty years earlier. If anything could unite the people and bring back the sense of community that had been lost, it had to be this.

But so much had changed; so much tradition forgotten; so many lives lost; so much suffering; so much hope deferred. Back then, Rebecca and her brothers had been too excited to sit down as they watched the proceedings. This time, Rebecca didn't have an assigned seat either and she had to remain standing for hours through the whole ceremony. Rebecca was not one to push herself forward and demand a seat, but from her vantage point, she had ample opportunity to watch the subtle manoeuvres for position going on with the endless speeches. It simply couldn't be as engaging to be standing for that long at her age as it had been at age ten!

The coronation had taken place, but what was next? Life began to settle back into its normal routine of survival. Just as it had been after independence in the 1960s, a tenuous cooperation developed in the 1990s between the Buganda government and the central government of President Yoweri Museveni. Some people tried to discourage the new leadership of Buganda, saying that the kingdom was no longer relevant, especially to the young people. Rebecca and the Prime Minister sat down to discuss her role. She was introduced to the newly appointed Minister for Culture and Tradition, Honourable Kayiira Gajuule, with whom she would be required to pursue the restoration of the cultural aspects of the kingdom. Although her role might be limited at first, they insisted that a plot of land be identified where they would start to build her palace and the new minister and the Katikkiro approached the Kabaka about it. The newly restored kingdom did not have enough resources to build her a new palace or support her financially, however, and what would rightfully have been the location of her palace was occupied by someone else.

There were several major functions that Rebecca had to attend with the Kabaka following his coronation: the opening of the palace at Mengo; the first session of parliament at Nsambya; the opening of the palace at Kako in Masaka; other religious and cultural events. She particularly enjoyed the annual clan football matches they attended together. Rebecca was initially not recognised as the Namasole (queen mother), despite the functions she had attended, until the new Prime Minister, Honourable Joseph Mulwanyammuli Ssemwogerere, introduced her to the Lukiiko (Buganda parliament). He insisted that she be properly introduced at every function she attended with the newly crowned Kabaka. They even had talks with the Katikkiro about restoring the Namasole's power as it had been in pre-colonial days, but that was only in jest. In those days, she would have been expected to advise the king in governing his kingdom. She would've been the only person allowed to discipline him and he would have had to come to her palace whenever summoned!

Rebecca had managed to remain incognito while the kingdom lay dormant for almost twenty years. Gone were the days when the Namasole had her own palace and wielded equal power to the Kabaka, having her own court, her own prime minister, her own set of chiefs and her own army. The 1900 agreement between the British colonial government and the Kabaka and his regents had dissolved that power in favour of the palace regents. The agreement did provide for the reigning queen mother to retain 16 square miles of her own property which was not subject to the government tax. She was also accorded an allowance of 50 pounds a year from

Her Majesty's government throughout her lifetime or until the reigning Kabaka's death, at which time a new queen mother would succeed.[6]

Rebecca adapted herself to her role as Namasole using her own resources. It must have appeared to outsiders that she was an independently wealthy widow, but she had long ago learnt to stretch her resources. She would keep her farm going but do everything in her power to support the newly restored kingdom. She also knew she would need to get advice from others. As her father had said to her aunts when they nominated her for the queen mother role, she had not been exposed to the traditions of the royal family in her youth. Secondly, after almost thirty years, many of those who had been at the centre of the kingdom had passed away. She *had* considered abdicating her role as queen mother when the pre-coronation rituals began. Some of the traditional rituals stood in direct contradiction to her Christian beliefs. It was only out of respect for the family honour that she did not.

Former Katikkiro Mulwanyammuli Ssemwogerere recalls of the Namasole in the early days: *"I myself was surprised and pleased by her behaviour. She was not well versed in Buganda culture, but she made every effort to do what she was supposed to do; despite her Western upbringing. She persevered, even though she was brought up privileged. That surprised me – her keenness to learn, in an environment in which many traditions had been forgotten. Those who knew them had passed away; so we had to study.*

We all believed the kingdom would be fully restored. Going around Buganda, people still loved their kingdom. She had a car and would provide her own petrol. Whether she sold land or cows, I don't know, but she did her duties for love of the kingdom. Even though she served the kingdom, her own work on her farm didn't suffer. She was very hardworking; she kept time like a European; she fulfilled whatever was expected of her. She loved the Kabaka a lot, but the way he's kept in the lubiri (palace), she had a hard time reaching him. Despite that, she never gave up hope and always tried to show him her love. She was always asking what could be done to make things better for him and for the kingdom.

She never flagged in zeal, even when things got tough. She looked kali (Swahili for severe), but she was very kind-hearted. Unless you got close to her, you would never know how kind, loving and giving she was. Despite all the struggles, she loved Ssabasajja Kabaka. For that reason, I loved her so much and I honour her. She and my mother, Nantale Mulwanya, also loved each other a lot. Because I am from the Lugave clan like her mother, she always referred to me as Kojja (maternal uncle)."

Rebecca's cousin, Ruth Mayanja-Nkangi recalls: *"When Rebecca became Namasole, I became a bit concerned for her. I knew how passionate she was about God and the things of God. I wondered how she was going to handle what was expected of her in that role. One day, I talked to her about it. She told me she was going to do it by spending more time with God in prayer and reading the Bible. And that's exactly what she did!"* She was like Naaman, commander of the Syrian army before Elisha the prophet in 2nd Kings, chapter 5, asking the Lord to forgive him for accompanying his master into the pagan temple of Rimmon. She knew that the Lord would pardon her in this thing.

Chapter Twenty-Four

The Fall

It was five years after her first visit that Rebecca took her second trip to America with her sister, Damallie. By this time, Philippa was living in Cleveland, Ohio with her son. She was doing a fellowship in Infectious Diseases. Bessie came up from Atlanta and they all drove up to Niagara Falls. It was an awesome sight, especially from the deck of the ferryboat ride they took down the river. The sight was well worth being drenched by the relentless spray, despite the raincoats they were given to wear. That winter, Rebecca experienced her first 'Northeaster'. She, Philippa and her son, Jeremiah, were driving from Cleveland to Washington, D.C. for the Thanksgiving holiday when it started snowing. The wind was howling and the snowdrifts were piling up higher than the cars. You could barely see the road or the car in front of you. They rode along slowly in Philippa's little car and made it in time for Thanksgiving dinner. And thankful they were! Bessie had just moved to Washington, D.C. She had finished her postgraduate training in Obstetrics and Gynaecology and was starting her first real job. That was another milestone for Rebecca. God had been faithful with that widow's purse.

By the time Rebecca returned to Uganda, she had been away in England for almost a year. She was just in time to welcome two new grandchildren into the world, Mbakire in Nairobi and Daudi in Kampala. That made ten grandchildren whom Latimer did not get to see. Now that she had two daughters living in Kampala with their families, Damallie and Becky, Rebecca could thoroughly enjoy her children and grandchildren. One of her granddaughters, Liza, was especially close to her grandmother. She would try to hide in Rebecca's car whenever she was leaving their house, hoping no one would notice and she could go and spend the night with grandma. Pauline and her brother, Philip, often visited their grandmother during their holidays. They loved to fall asleep in her bed. Rebecca would wake them up at 5:30 am after she had said her prayers and done her morning exercise. Then she would drag them down to the milking shed, still half asleep, so that they could help milk the cows. That was fun for them, once they were awake. After breakfast, she would pile her grandchildren into her car and take them into town.

Family was as important to Rebecca as ever and she insisted that they visit the children's other grandparents as well. Frequently, she would stop by her dear friend Agnes's house. She was now in a wheelchair and less mobile. Rebecca would help her into the car and take her to her doctor's appointments. It was a constant reminder to give thanks for her own good health. After running around with her grandchildren and attending to the afternoon chores on the farm, Rebecca would be too tired in the evening to do much more than sit knitting while the grandchildren jabbered away. At bedtime, she repeated the timeless bedtime stories she had heard from her parents and told countless times to her own children. They particularly liked the story of the silverback mountain gorilla because she always spoke in a deep, scary voice when speaking for him. She was ever the doting grandmother, but glad to give the children back to their parents when their visits ended. She would say "kawuna" and then, "I love you" as she waved goodbye.

Rebecca had always been the picture of health, as active as she was. Her sister had come to spend her summer holidays with her in July 1997 and they returned to England together at the end of her holidays. The day after they arrived, the British Prime Minister announced the tragic death of Princess Diana in a fatal car accident. It was followed by the death of Mother Teresa of Calcutta a week later. Rebecca had admired both women's work and agreed with those who referred to Diana as the 'Queen of hearts' and Mother Teresa as 'Queen of the poor.' Rebecca couldn't help but remember her own school days in India working with the poor during her social studies course. In September, there was a celebration of the Kingdom of Buganda in London and both she and the Kabaka were in attendance. It was not long after that that her royal 'son' rang to advise her of the death of his step grandmother, Uncle Christopher's South African wife, Pumla. Rebecca could do no more than express her condolences. She was getting ready to travel to America to spend Christmas with Bessie and her new husband, Charles.

It was one week before her scheduled date of departure. Rebecca's sister, Damallie, was away at school and Rebecca was busying herself with the laundry. Damallie was always reminding her that she was on holiday and she should take it easy, but Rebecca was not one to sit around twiddling her thumbs. Her sister recounts the details:

"During that particular holiday Mama (Rebecca) was very strong and healthy. Each morning after I left to go to work, she would get up and make her breakfast and prepare things to eat and little bits of food to take to the homeless who lived under the Waterloo Bridge. I used to worry because some were junkies on drugs. I warned her about it, but she said no harm could come to her. When she finished handing out food to these people and having a chat with them, she would go around to museums or other places of interest. Days/ weeks before her accident, I suggested that she should have my

school address and phone number in case she needed me or for an emergency. We decided to place one of the cards we wrote in the coat she used to wear and one upstairs in her bedroom on her chest of drawers.

That day was Friday, because that is when she liked to do our washing, in spite of me asking her to do it on Saturday when we were together. I also asked her to throw the washing down the stairs, instead of carrying it in the hamper as we did not have a banister on the left hand side. She had a lovely blue denim skirt she often wore which, when she came down the stairs, she seemed to tread in it."

Accidents always seem to happen in slow motion. Rebecca could remember tripping, reaching out for the banister that was not there, and then seeing the floor rising towards her for what seemed an eternity. The searing pain that shot through her left shoulder hit her squarely and jolted her back into real time. She lay motionless for a few minutes as the pain registered in her mind. Her arm must be broken, but she wondered if anything else was. She knew she had not hit her head because she was conscious throughout the fall. She tried to move her hand but her arm was not communicating with her fingers or her elbow. She realised she had broken it, so she pushed herself up the stairs and crawled to her bedroom, where she found the card with the details of Damallie's school.

Damallie's narrative continues:

"Fortunately, we had also put a phone extension in her room. She rang the school. Everybody knew who she was. The secretary told her that I was teaching but as she sounded stressed, she asked Mama what was wrong. Mama insisted on talking to me. The secretary went and told the headmistress, who went and covered my class while I talked to Mama in the office. She told me she felt like she might have broken her arm. Typical of her, she was apologising for the inconvenience. I

told her to go downstairs and wait in the front room by the phone while I went back and talked to the headmistress.

The headmistress instructed the secretary to ring for an ambulance and went and found another teacher to take my class while I went home to wait with Mama for the ambulance. By the time I got home, she had been collected by the ambulance. I phoned the school as I did not know which hospital they had taken her to. They said the ambulance men had used Mama's card in her coat to ring and tell the school that they were taking her to Ealing Hospital. That is where I drove to and found her waiting for the consultant. By now, she was in quite a bit of pain but it was me who was crying uncontrollably. We wanted her to have a plaster cast placed on her arm but the consultant refused and suggested Mama wear a sling and take pain killers. When we told him that in less than two weeks she was going to America, he refused to let her travel, stating that the air pressure might cause more damage to her arm. We begged, but he refused and said he wanted to see her in a week's time.

Mama and I felt that maybe we could still go and begged my own doctor to try and get the consultant to change his mind. She told us to keep the follow up appointment but not to let on that Mama was going to go ahead and go to America. She said Mama should go and enjoy her Christmas. She could see the consultant again when she came back. We were worried about her not getting the plaster cast but my doctor explained that it was better; otherwise Mama's arm would not heal straight. It would heal in the shape of the plaster cast like Daddy's had. She said not to worry about the other doctor/ consultant and not to tell him where Mama had been when she came back."

Damallie made sure Rebecca received special attention during her air travel, complete with a wheelchair in both airports. Rebecca wondered what the first meeting with her son-in-law would be like; the only time she was without pain was after a heavy dose of pain medicine. But she needn't have worried. Her daughter and her new son-in-law welcomed her with open arms, and when Bessie was away at work, her husband, Charles, was as attentive a caretaker as any nurse could have been. A follow-up X-ray showed that the arm was healing properly, and gradually, she needed less and less pain medicine. Rebecca was not one to complain, but she thought often about the time when Latimer had broken his arm in the car accident thirty years earlier. Ten years later he had broken his leg in another accident. Empathy was a virtue Rebecca already possessed, but she certainly developed a deeper understanding of the suffering caused by intense physical pain.

Grandson Jeremiah joined them for the Christmas holiday. Snowfall did not stop them from going around the city to admire the Christmas lights. Ten days later, there was another piece of exciting news from Kampala: the birth of another grandchild, Catherine, on January 4th. She had missed that birth, though. When Rebecca was well enough, Charles and Bessie took her and a couple of their friends on a trip to New England. It took eight hours by car to get to Boston. The next day, they drove to Bessie's alma mater, Wellesley College. There Rebecca met her daughter's former Dean, Pamela Daniels, who had been like a mother to Bessie as she adjusted to life in America during her freshman year. While they were in Boston, Rebecca had another experience she would never forget: attending a Christian crusade with thousands of people in a huge auditorium that could seat twenty thousand people. They were all glorifying God. This must be what heaven would be like: people of all ages, races, denominations and languages praising their Creator. The presence of God was tangible; many were being healed of various physical ailments; others, like Rebecca, received comfort and encouragement to go home and face the challenges still ahead of them.

Chapter Twenty-Five

Royal Wedding

Rebecca's brothers had painfully wrested the executive powers of attorney of their father's estate from her after several years of wrangling. Her children and her sister encouraged her to give up those powers for the sake of peace in the family. Her brothers immediately set off selling the land that Rebecca's father had wanted to preserve for his grandchildren. They ran into a network of crooked schemes while trying to sell the land that landed them all in and out of court. While she was away in England, Rebecca had given the powers of administration of her property to a cousin. This cousin and the surveyor had sold several plots of land on her behalf, but the figures didn't quite add up. It was several more years before Rebecca figured out that an elaborate, fraudulent scheme of operations had developed involving surveyors, potential land buyers and the land title office. The celebrated new regime had brought the longed-for peace and security, but the insidious disease of corruption was spreading like a contagious virus. It had morphed from a seemingly harmless means of survival under Idi Amin to a crippling systemic disease that was infecting all facets of the society. It was like gangrene, spreading from one tiny wound to reach the rest of the body.

The year 1999 promised to be a banner year. It began inauspiciously, however, with several members of the royal family declaring their doubts that Kabaka Ronald Muwenda Mutebi II was really the son of his father, the late Kabaka Sir Edward Mutesa II, and suggesting that he was the son of a rival suitor of his mother. Rebecca was at a loss for how to respond to this new crisis. To respond would be to legitimise their claims in some way and compromise the honour of her cousin. The Katikkiro (Prime Minister) called the parliament together on the 20th of January and the parliament announced that there was no question in their minds that the Kabaka was the rightful heir to the throne of his father. Rebecca and the rest of his mother's family were relieved when the furore died down and those responsible melted back into the shadows.

On Valentine's Day, February 14th, the Kabaka called a few of his trusted friends and family to his palace in Banda and introduced them to his fiancée, Sylvia Nagginda, daughter of Mr. Luswata Ssebugwawo. Rebecca was so happy for the Kabaka; the kingdom was beginning to wonder whether he would ever find a suitable queen. When Rebecca asked for the name of the mother of the queen-to-be, she was told, "Her name is Rebecca Musoke and she lives in New York." Rebecca did a double take; the two mothers-in-law would have the same name! Sylvia was returning to America after the introduction, so Rebecca gave her Bessie's phone number so that they could meet.

The parliament was agog with excitement and serious discussions were held to determine where the reigning Namasole's oft-discussed palace should be built. They determined that it should be built for her on the Kabaka's land at Bumbu, in Kitezi. Rebecca didn't concern herself much with the plans; it wasn't *her* idea to build herself a palace. But one day she decided to stop by the construction site. She couldn't believe her eyes: the plans called for just two small rooms. Rebecca knew it wouldn't do justice to the Kabaka's send-off.

Rebecca and the Minister for Culture and Tradition, Omutaka Kayiira, went back to the Katikkiro and had him revise the plans for the palace. In his benevolence, he did provide doors and windows for the new palace, but Rebecca had to drive up and down looking for bags of cement; a rare commodity in those days. One of the neighbours donated his tractor for the clearing of the land around the construction site and other neighbours gave them access to water and toilets.

The Kabaka's grandfather's (Uncle Christopher's) last funeral rites were performed that June. Only then could preparations begin in earnest for the royal wedding, which was to be held in August. Rebecca had to make multiple visits to the Katikkiro with the Minister for Culture and Tradition to discuss the on-going plans. It helped that she and the Katikkiro had become good friends. She also had to meet with the other Namasoles to get their advice. In July, they performed the requisite traditional rituals. One of the functions Rebecca had to fulfil was to locate the 'Omulongo' ('twin' or umbilical cord) of the Kabaka. Rebecca had no idea where it was and how she was supposed to find it. She and the faithful Minister for Culture and Tradition had driven from county to county, searching for the artefacts required to perform the rituals and often returning home after midnight.

Philippa had returned from America in 1995 and started working for the Department of Paediatrics and Child Health at Makerere University. Rebecca was so proud of her when, several years later, she stepped into her father's shoes and became head of the department. Philippa did not approve of her mother's stepped up schedule and informed the minister of this. But Rebecca was never one to excuse herself if she felt something was her duty, or someone else needed her help. She plodded on.

Rebecca fell deathly ill later that month. One morning she woke up feeling dizzy, but she made light of it when she rang her daughter, telling her she was just a little tired. Later that day, her brother, Myers, rang Philippa to tell her that her mother was lethargic and disoriented. Philippa rushed over to her mother's side to take her to the doctor. Rebecca was diagnosed with cerebral malaria and admitted to hospital to be administered intravenous (IV) antimalarial medicine. It required several days of IV therapy. When she was discharged from hospital, her daughter took her home to her own house to help her recover from the illness. As soon as she was well enough, Rebecca continued her duties preparing for the wedding.

On August 25th, two days before the wedding, Rebecca cooked a final meal for her 'son'. She was given a cow, goats and chickens for the feast, but she had to provide the matoke (plantains) and other ingredients, banana leaves, pots and pans, firewood and water for the occasion. It was a huge feast attended by hundreds of people. The traditional drums had only arrived that day, but they rang out the 'mubala' (drumbeats) of 'Buganda Buladde' (All is well in Buganda) and 'Kuzaala Kujagana' (A joyful occasion) in unified solidarity. Her 'palace' at Bumbu was just a half-finished shell, but Rebecca successfully performed the pre-wedding ceremonies in it anyway. There was no electricity, so they used hand-held lanterns. There were no panes in the windows, so they simply covered them with curtains. The roof wasn't quite finished, so they used the extra corrugated iron sheets to build a makeshift toilet. Thankfully, it didn't rain that night.

Rebecca sat on the floor so that the Kabaka could sit on her lap, take a morsel of food from her hand and be instructed that he could no longer come to his 'mother' for food and counsel; he must now rely on his wife. She sat on that cold, hard, cement slab for hours and felt chilled to the bone. After the ceremony, she and the other ladies slept on the floor of the crowded front 'room'. Rebecca woke up in the middle of the night with severe cramps in her legs. Her nieces massaged her legs to relieve the cramps. She felt life seep back into her body. The others all suggested that she spend the rest of the night in her car. The next day, her daughters took her to a doctor. She had never had diabetes or high blood pressure, but her blood pressure was high. The doctor wanted to admit her to hospital again, but Rebecca refused. She said, "Doctor, I have important functions to attend."

They had promised Rebecca a van to transport her and her family to the wedding ceremonies. Instead, they sent a regular car with a driver. She, her sister Damallie, Bessie and other family members rode together to Namirembe Cathedral. President Yoweri Museveni had been invited to the wedding, so security was tight. Everyone was being instructed to get out of their cars at the bottom of the hill, and despite the driver's declaration that he ought to be allowed to transport the queen mother all the way up to the cathedral, they were turned away. Rebecca and the others disembarked and walked the rest of the way up the hill. That was painful for Rebecca, but at least, when they did get inside the cathedral, they had a place for her to sit behind the choir. Those who had accompanied her had to fend for themselves, so Damallie came up and sat on the stairs by her feet. She wasn't going to leave her sister alone, even for a minute, after all she had already been through.

After the wedding ceremony, they walked back to where the driver had parked the car. The wedding reception was to be on the Mengo Palace grounds not far away, but because of the thronging crowds of people and all the cars, it was a slow, painstaking journey. At the gate, they were almost turned away again, but one of the ladies from Kasubi recognised Rebecca and informed the guards that she was the Namasole. They were ushered in. At first, they were all seated in the tent outside; later, an usher came and took Rebecca inside the palace. She was seated at the high table, next to Mr. and Mrs. Sebuggwawo, Sylvia's grandparents, and the mother of the bride, Mrs. Rebecca Musoke. They were good company and Rebecca could always converse easily with anyone, but she wasn't feeling well and she missed having her sister nearby. When the ceremonies were over, the driver did his duty and drove Rebecca and her family home. At least she didn't have to walk home like she had to fifty years earlier when she waited on her cousin Damali. When the rest of Kabaka Mutesa's wedding party were leaving for the post-reception festivities, young Rebecca was told to go home. She had gladly taken off her shoes to relieve her aching feet and walked home all alone.

Despite all the obstacles and battles with illness, Rebecca was gratified: Ronnie was married! The day after the wedding, Rebecca cooked a meal for the newly-weds and she and the rest of the family took it over to the palace at Kireka. They waited for two hours before the Kabaka and the Nnabagereka (queen) came out to see them. By this time, Rebecca had had to leave; she was still unwell from the ceremonies she had performed in the stark, unfinished palace. She left the rest of the family to serve the meal. Several days later, they returned 'okujja Omugole mukisenge' (to take the bride out of the bedroom, a traditional ceremony signifying the beginning of the marriage). Rebecca cooked every known traditional food for the bride and, during the ceremony, demonstrated to her how it should be cooked. In turn, the bride's mother invited them all over for a meal before she left for her home in America. Rebecca promised to visit her new 'sister-in-law' in New York on her next overseas trip.

Rebecca was invited to the palace festivities to welcome in the new millennium with the Kabaka and the Nnabagereka. Her public role was now largely ceremonial, however. Rebecca was not expected to advise the king in the governance of his kingdom; neither could she advise him in personal matters. As she reflected on the year and its accomplishments, Rebecca couldn't help but remember that she had also lost so many friends and relatives: the Namasole of Kasubi, the Kabaka's uncle Kungu (Uncle Christopher's son), Latimer's nephew Eddie Kamanyi, son-in-law George Mugabi (daughter Eva had passed away two years earlier), Mrs. Kabali and her daughter Mary, sister-in-law Mrs. Kinatama, brother-in-law Mr. Sempira, Professor Sekabunga, the husband of her close friend Agnes ... none of them made it into the new millennium; but here she was, about to turn sixty-eight and as 'fit-as-a-fiddle'. Despite a few illnesses that she could attribute to stress associated with her official duties, she was strong and healthy. Whether or not she was always recognised as the Namasole, for her own family, for their friends, for the families of her friends and employees, for people she met all around the kingdom, she *truly* was the beloved reigning matriarch. Her children would urge her to visit them around the world as often as she could.

Chapter Twenty-Six

Royal Baby

It was December of 2000 and Rebecca was preparing to travel again. She was in a dilemma. The Nnabagereka, Sylvia, was with child and due the following July, but Rebecca needed to go to America in April or May to be present for the birth of her own grandchild. She went to Bulange (the parliament building) and notified the Prime Minister that she was leaving the country. She was advised that unless she was present for the birth of the royal child, its legitimacy and right to the throne might be questioned. Thankfully, Sylvia was planning to deliver her baby in London. Rebecca travelled through London to America in April with a sad heart that year. Her daughter had just lost her baby and there was little that Rebecca could do but be there for her and try to comfort her. She wished that she could stay longer, but by the middle of June she was back in England, awaiting the arrival of the next prince or princess of Buganda.

Rebecca kept herself busy during the day preparing meals and doing the household chores she loved to do. She was knitting a little sweater for the prince or princess. Damallie came home early from school whenever she didn't have a meeting so that she could be with Rebecca. After supper in the evening, they would sit down and chitchat while Damallie was marking her pupils' schoolwork. Rebecca would help out by mounting the children's artwork on backing paper and even going over their spelling and maths for Damallie. She didn't discuss her feelings about the loss of her grandchild, but Damallie knew that she was grieving and suggested that she return to the U.S. to be with her daughter. Rebecca said, "No, I can't go back; the Nnabagereka's baby is due any day now."

She had never been present for the birth of a royal child, so Rebecca spent hours on the phone trying to figure out exactly what her role was expected to be. No one else seemed sure either because most of them had been quite young the last time there had been an heir to the throne born into the royal family. It was like the blind leading the blind. They heard that the Nnabagereka had arrived in the country and were able to arrange a visit with the mother-to-be on July 1st. The planned delivery date arrived and Rebecca was still not sure in which hospital the baby was to be born. Her friend, Auntie Ruth, picked Rebecca up from the house (Damallie was away at school) and promised to deliver her to the expected venue come hell or high water. They located the Queen Charlotte Hospital in London, but were barred from entering the maternity ward. By the time they were escorted onto the ward, the delivery had already taken place. Rebecca and Auntie Ruth Senkatuka were delighted to welcome the baby princess into the world. She placed a call to Uganda to the new father to congratulate him, but was disappointed when she was unable to speak to him.

The baby princess was born on July 4, 2001. Rebecca was instructed to choose a Nabikande (royal midwife) from her family who would look after the newborn. The royal family suggested her sister Damallie, but Rebecca wouldn't hear of it. Her sister was too busy to abandon her teaching job or take up any additional duties. She was in the middle of switching schools that summer. There was some back and forth discussion, but they finally picked someone acceptable to both sides. Meanwhile, there was a rumour floating around that Rebecca had been hospitalised with severe hypertension. When her daughters rang from Kampala, Rebecca reassured them that she was well. And she was, physically, but Damallie knew that she really wished that she was in America, comforting her daughter, instead of being where she was. She would often wake up at night and find Rebecca's light on. When she walked in, Rebecca would be praying or reading her Bible. Damallie was relieved when Philippa came through London on her way to the U.S. that summer and spent a few days with her mother. Spending time with her close family and friends was definitely helping her recover her usual buoyant personality.

Rebecca was visiting the new princess and her mother one day when suddenly the Nnabagereka shouted, "Mama, Mama, come and see!" Rebecca went into the next room and looked at what Sylvia was pointing to. On the television screen, there was a skyscraper with smoke billowing from its side. The building next to it also had smoke spiralling out of it, but higher up. Rebecca asked what had happened and Sylvia explained that the BBC was reporting that two aeroplanes had crashed into the Twin Towers in New York City. When the first plane crashed into the first tower, everyone thought it was an accident. Now that a second plane had also crashed, people were starting to suspect that it was not a coincidence. Rebecca sat down next to Sylvia and, with their eyes glued to the television screen, they tried to decipher what was going on in America. They were showing crowds of people running away from the smouldering buildings and a short while later, they were showing clouds of black smoke billowing from the Pentagon in Washington, D.C. They both had loved ones in New York and Washington, so they watched with growing concern.

Sylvia left the room to go and nurse the baby while Rebecca kept a vigilant watch on the television. A short while later, they watched in horror as one of the towers collapsed and disappeared under a cloud of debris. Thirty minutes later, the second tower also collapsed. They could not reach anyone they knew in New York or Washington, D.C. They could only pray and hope that their loved ones were all right as the nightmare unfolded before their very eyes. Would that it *was* just a bad dream from which they would awake and find that the world had not really gone mad. The newscasters were reporting that it was terrorism; that the aeroplanes had been hijacked and deliberately flown into the towers and into the Pentagon; that another plane had crashed before it reached the White House; that thousands of innocent Americans may have been killed... Thankfully, the next day they both heard from their loved ones: everyone was safe, but the world had changed forever.

Rebecca's next trip to America was in June 2002. Sadly, Rebecca had just lost her best friend, Agnes. Agnes's children would forever be grateful for all that Rebecca had done for their mother; but Rebecca could never forget that Agnes had stood by her during the most difficult period of her life and become a lifelong friend. She mourned her friend's passing. Two days after arriving in London, Rebecca and Damallie went to visit their cousin, Duncan, who had recently had surgery on his leg, a consequence of long-standing diabetes. Two weeks later, they were on a plane to the U.S. Bessie had invited her mother and her Aunt Damallie to visit them again. Things had certainly changed since Rebecca and Damallie's last trip to the U.S. together in 2000. There were long lines at the security checkpoint in the airport; there were soldiers with guns dotted around the airport; there were more policemen visible on the streets.

Rebecca's son-in-law had advised her to get a Canadian visa before she left Uganda because they were planning a road trip across the border. Their hosts had hired a van and they drove through most of the Northeast of the United States on the way to Montreal, Canada. In Montreal, they stayed with Bessie's best friend from college, Samar. She was living with her brother, mother and aunt who had all emigrated from Palestine. They took them to visit the historic St. Joseph's Oratory Church while touring the city.

The round trip took them through Toronto. The next day they drove to Niagara Falls. Rebecca and Damallie had been to the American side of the falls seven years earlier, but the sight from the Canadian side was even more breath-taking. You could stand right next to the edge of the falls and see the water as it began its deafening cascade over the rugged edge of the cliff. You could feel the spray from the turbulent waters bouncing off your face and cooling you down. If you closed your eyes, the sound of the rushing waters would transport you to another place and time; you could imagine you were there when Moses stretched out his hand and divided the waters of the Red Sea; or even imagine being there when God divided the waters below the firmament and created the dry land. It was hard to tear themselves away, get back into the metal box on wheels and drive away.

Rebecca was still as adventurous as ever. She enjoyed driving home through the mountains and then going down to the beach on the Atlantic Ocean. It was intriguing to realise that the waves she was watching may have originated on the west coast of the very African continent from which she had come. She had travelled by ship across the Indian Ocean herself many years ago, but she couldn't imagine crossing such a vast ocean in the belly of a slave ship. She had great admiration for those who had made it. Rebecca's major interest had always been in people. Sitting on the beach chatting with her sister gave her ample opportunity to watch them. Some were paddling in the shallow water, some were further out riding the waves ashore, some were building castles in the sand and some were just lying there soaking it all in. She wouldn't have dreamt of putting on a swimming suit or getting into the water herself now and she laughed when her daughter suggested it. But Americans of all ages and sizes were unselfconsciously walking half-naked along the entire beach and the boardwalk.

Rebecca took a long walk by herself early one morning. She had left her sister, daughter, son-in-law and their friend asleep in the cottage and walked straight down the main street of Ocean City. The road was perfectly straight with each cross street running perpendicular to it at regular intervals. Rebecca was quite sure she couldn't get lost. She looked at the quaint little houses on one side of the street, opposite all the hotels facing the ocean on the other side. She could hear the sound of the waves of the high tide crashing onto the empty beach in the distance. She reached the point where the cross street was that would take you back over the bridge to the mainland. Rebecca felt she had gone far enough; she turned around and started walking back to their rented cottage. She had counted the number of cross streets as she passed them but when she got to 17, the cottage wasn't there! She walked another couple of blocks, but there was no sight of the light blue cottage.

Rebecca was lost and she didn't know the address of the place where they were staying, but she didn't panic. This was a civilised country; it was broad daylight by now and there must be a police station somewhere. That thought had just crossed her mind when she saw a policeman approaching her. Rebecca lost no time in telling him she had lost her way. He asked her if she had a key to the cottage she had left that morning. Rebecca replied that of course she did; how was she supposed to get back in with everyone else sleeping? The officer asked to see the key. Rebecca handed it to him and he turned it over. There on the back of the key was the full address of the cottage! It wasn't far from where they were standing, on a parallel street. Apparently, Rebecca had walked back along a parallel street but had not realised it. When the officer got her home, the whole family was up looking for her. They teased her all the way home, suggesting that she leave a trail of breadcrumbs the next time she wanted to go exploring on her own!

Their next trip was to New York. After paying a visit to the Nnabagereka's mother, Mrs. Rebecca Musoke, Rebecca and

Damallie were able to spend some time with their paternal Aunt Race Kanyike who had settled in New York over thirty years earlier. She was living there with her daughter and two grandchildren. She was the last surviving child of their grandmother, Damali Nalule, who had passed away before either Rebecca or Damallie were born. They reminisced over old times and their aunt expressed her wish to be buried in the land she had adopted as her own. They took a tour of Manhattan and saw ground zero, where the Twin Towers had once stood. It was sad to see the pictures of those who had perished and read the farewell notes of their loved ones that were posted on the nearby notice board. Where the towers once stood was now just a gaping hole filled with construction equipment. There were crowds of tourists milling around, but all were in reverent silence. It was a relief to leave downtown Manhattan and explore other parts of New York City.

Chapter Twenty-Seven

Confusion

Rebecca returned to England to spend the winter months of 2002 with her sister. Cousin Pumlet came and spent four days with them over the Christmas holiday. On Christmas day, they all went over to Adam's house to celebrate. On New Year's Eve, the family at home rang to wish them a happy new year. Rebecca's two eldest grandchildren had both graduated from high school with honours: Pauline was going to study law at Makerere University and Jeremiah had been awarded a scholarship to study music at the University of Kentucky! As usual, Rebecca kept herself busy over the next weeks talking to family and friends, writing letters, knitting, cooking and entertaining visitors. But she yearned for the outdoors.

One day, the sun did more than just peep out from behind the clouds. It was shining bright enough that you could feel the warmth by the window. Rebecca donned her winter coat, unlocked the front door and stepped outside to test the air. The wind was calm and she really didn't feel cold at all. She decided to take a brisk walk around the neighbourhood. She was still a pretty fast walker, so it didn't take her long to do her usual walk; but by the time she came back to Framfield Road she had started to feel the chill in the air. She had also forgotten to take her hat and gloves with her, so her ears and fingertips were tingling. She was glad to unlock the front door and step back into the nice, warm living room.

The next day, Rebecca had a mild cough and told Damallie she thought she was coming down with a cold. Damallie encouraged her to take the usual home remedies: drink plenty of warm liquids, bundle yourself up and stay indoors! She went off to school. Rebecca did as she was told and slept most of the day. When she woke up, she was feeling much better. She drank some warm tea and ate a little food. They spent the evening chatting away as Damallie marked her pupils' homework. The next morning, Rebecca felt feverish and asked Damallie to check her temperature. It was high. And she was still coughing. After drinking her morning tea and taking some Panadol, she insisted that Damallie go on to school. Rebecca never would let anyone fuss over her own health; but a little while later, she wished maybe she *hadn't* been so cavalier. She was starting to feel some discomfort in her chest whenever she took a deep breath. And she was dizzy when she tried to get up and go to the kitchen. She decided to stay put on the living room sofa.

When Damallie walked into the house that evening, all the lights were off. She wondered if Rebecca had decided to go to bed early and tiptoed around the house for a few minutes. She had taken off her coat and boots and put some groceries away in the kitchen before she realised that Rebecca was lying on the living room sofa. She decided to let her sleep on. Usually by this time Rebecca would have supper ready. Damallie went into the kitchen and started preparing their evening meal. While she was in the kitchen, Auntie Ruth rang and Rebecca picked up the phone in the living room. After speaking to Rebecca for a few minutes, she insisted on speaking to Damallie. Auntie Ruth was a doctor. She advised Damallie that her sister really wasn't well and she should get her some antibiotics. By this time, all the pharmacies were closed, so Damallie promised to obtain a prescription from her brother in the morning.

First thing in the morning, Damallie obtained the antibiotics and gave Rebecca her first dose. Rebecca wasn't feeling well, but again she insisted that her sister go on to school, now that she had the medicine she needed. Damallie left her with a warm drink in the flask and some food that she could easily heat up later. When Damallie returned, she found Rebecca asleep on the sofa again. She was rousable but felt very warm and her skin was clammy. Damallie sat her up and asked her how she was feeling. She could barely make out what she was saying, but she gathered that Rebecca was too weak and dizzy to walk to the kitchen so she hadn't eaten her lunch; her chest hurt when she coughed and so did her head. Damallie became alarmed, though, when some of the things Rebecca was saying did not make sense. She was talking about getting into her car and driving back to the farm. It was a Friday evening and Damallie thought that her sister's condition might deteriorate over the weekend. She suggested to Rebecca that she ring the doctor, but Rebecca would not hear of it.

By Sunday evening, it was becoming obvious that the antibiotics were not working. Damallie took Rebecca to see the doctor the next morning. Damallie's own doctor was on holiday, but one of the other doctors was happy to see her. Rebecca was chatty as she always was at the doctor's office and she convinced the doctor that her condition wasn't serious. Damallie took her sister home, made sure she was comfortable and then rushed off to school. That afternoon, she rang to check on her sister. Rebecca appeared to be getting more and more confused by the hour. Damallie rushed back home and tried to reach her doctor's office. They were closed, so Damallie rang the emergency number. They promised that a doctor would be there in 30 to 60 minutes.

Damallie was in a dilemma. She was waiting for a callback from the doctor to confirm her address. Bessie had learnt of her mother's condition when she rang and talked to her mother. She had notified other members of the family of Rebecca's confused state of mind. They started ringing one after the other, tying up the line. Some of them were wondering why she wasn't taking Rebecca to hospital. They didn't understand that going to casualty when you are not in an emergency could be a disaster. You could wait for hours for some attention and then simply be told to go home and see your doctor in the morning. Finally, there was a knock on the door and Damallie was relieved to see the doctor standing outside the door. He examined Rebecca thoroughly and quickly made the diagnosis of pneumonia. Her confusion was due to lack of oxygen to her brain from her compromised lungs. He prescribed her a heavy dose of antibiotics, more Panadol and a sedative to help her sleep.

The next day, Adam came over to look after his mother while Damallie went to school. It took a week of antibiotics before Rebecca was strong enough to leave the living room sofa and go back to sleeping in her bedroom upstairs. Contributing to Damallie's anxiety were the endless phone calls and grandmother's remedies being suggested for Rebecca. Some even suggested that because she was so busy, perhaps Rebecca should board a plane and return to Uganda where there would be more people to take care of her! Damallie didn't appreciate that suggestion, knowing that her sister was too weak to travel and remembering what had happened to her father on his final trip.

Three weeks into her illness, Rebecca's condition was improving. Damallie's doctor had returned by then and they both felt like she was now in caring, competent hands. She had finished her course of antibiotics and her chest did not hurt when she coughed any more. Her X-ray was clear and she could breathe more freely and painlessly. But Rebecca would never forget that feeling of air hunger she had experienced and knew her asthmatic children had experienced many times in their lives. By now there were definitely signs that she was feeling better. She wrote some letters and started knitting a little jumper for a friend's grandchild. One day, when Damallie came home from school, she showed her the jumper and also gave her a card thanking her for taking care of her throughout her illness. Damallie simply burst into tears. She had been so afraid that she might lose her only sister and best friend, but had done everything she could *not* to reveal the depth of her anxiety to Rebecca. They knelt down and thanked God together.

Rebecca recovered completely from her bout of pneumonia and was careful not to venture out too far the rest of the winter. In March 2003 she took another short trip to America. She was nervous because President George W. Bush and Prime Minister Blair had just declared war on Iraq. But her journey was uneventful and she welcomed in the springtime in Washington, D.C. She had never been there at the beginning of spring and was mesmerised by the rebirth of all the flora and fauna. It was amazing to watch as 'dead' branches on trees and shrubs stuck out tiny, little leaves, then pretty little flowers of all colours of the rainbow. The most beautiful sight was the rows and rows of cherry blossoms lining the streets of Washington, D.C. that had been donated to America by Japan. Finally, the whole world turned a deep, rich shade of green. There were squirrels running around on the ground and hopping from tree branch to tree branch; there were rabbits and chipmunks peeping in and out and then scurrying away at the sound of humans; there were deer with their fawns wandering unabashedly through the back yard (compound). It almost reminded her of life on the farm.

Upon her return to England, Rebecca was busy. On the first Sunday of each month, they attended the Luganda service at St. John's Church in Waterloo; she and friend Kit took several sightseeing trips, including one to the Second World War cabinet war room of Winston Churchill; she had a visit with her long-time friends, the Stanfields; both Philippa and Becky stopped by London on their way home from trips to other parts of the world. Rebecca returned to Uganda that summer in time to attend the ten-year anniversary celebration of the restoration of the Kingdom of Buganda. It was a grand affair. Not long after that, she was surprised to get a ring from the Nnabagereka's (Queen's) secretary. The queen wanted to schedule a date to visit her at home.

Rebecca was surprised and pleased when she stopped by a few days later bringing the little princess with her. They had a cordial visit, exchanging pleasantries, sharing a meal and finally taking pictures of the princess with her royal 'grandmother'. Before she left, the Nnabagereka asked Rebecca if she would perform the traditional ceremonies that confirm the legitimacy of the Kabaka's children, usually performed by the paternal grandmother. The ceremony is called 'Okwalula Abaana' and is the traditional equivalent of today's DNA paternity testing.

The ceremony involves several members of the family. The children's mother brings the Balongo (dried umbilical cords) of her children, which she has kept since their births, to the paternal grandmother. The grandmother then smears the umbilical cords with cow butter and marks them so that the one belonging to each child is verifiable. After that, the grandmother places them in a basket containing water, milk and beer. If the child's umbilical cord floats, the clan elders declare that the child is legitimate, but if the cord sinks, the child is considered born out of adultery and disowned. The mother is in deep trouble and is urged to name the child's real father.

When the child passes the ritual test, the child is officially accepted into the family and the clan. The mother is also honoured as a faithful wife and mother. The converse is true of a child who does not pass the test: they and their mother are no longer respected by the family and the child is considered clanless. Clearly, the results could be skewed by a paternal grandmother who dislikes or distrusts her daughter-in-law!

Although it may not have been based on rigorous scientific evidence, the fear of having one's child fail their paternity test must have kept many a mother in line.

Rebecca cast her mind back to the last time she had been asked to perform this ritual. She had had to verify the Kabaka's legitimacy to the throne before he could take a Nnabagereka. Finding the object (Omulongo) required for the ceremony back then hadn't been easy, but she and Omutaka Kayiira (the Minister for Culture and Tradition) had enlisted the help of the Kabaka's lubuga (sister) and the Namasole of Kanyanya. They had had to find the Kimbugwe (keeper of the royal umbilical cord) and be directed to its location; they were then able to produce the verifiable goods.

The ceremony for the Kabaka's children was appropriately held at Kasubi where their ancestors are buried. This time, all the Balongo were duly produced. When the little princess's test took a little longer than the others, Rebecca counselled the judges to wait: she had been born miles away and deserved the extra time. She almost danced a jig when her confidence was rewarded! Rebecca was getting ready to leave when someone told her she ought to spend the night. She was confused because one of the other Namasoles had told her, a long time ago, she should never spend the night at the Kasubi Tombs: her 'husbands' (the late kings) 'lived' there and they would cause her to suffer. Whose advice should she follow? This time, Rebecca bowed to pressure and spent the night there. The next morning, she got up to leave and fell down as she tried to walk out. She was picked up and carried to her car. Then she started vomiting and was discovered to have a high fever. As usual, Rebecca had put duty before herself, unaware that her health was suffering.

Rebecca was determined to shield her children and grandchildren from the effects of her duties and they did not accompany her to the ceremonies. Those in the palace and parliament who did not appreciate her outspokenness did nothing to curb Rebecca's indomitable spirit. She had always felt indebted to the Namasoles of Mpererwe and Kanyanya for their guidance in the early days and to her sister-in-law, Kezia, who accompanied her to many of the functions. She often sat at the kingdom functions for hours in the burning sun, without food or water and she would get severely dehydrated. She could not get up to relieve herself during the ceremonies and her bladder paid the price. Women her age often have oversensitive bladders. Because she did not sleep well at night, she would often be too tired to be attentive through the endless speeches; then she would nod off. It was all that Kezia and her friend, Alice Sekagya, could do to keep her going.

Chapter Twenty-Eight

Mama Bash

Sadly, when Rebecca took her next trip to America it was to bid a final farewell to her Aunt Race. She had passed away in New York in the middle of 2005. When Rebecca and Damallie returned to Kampala at the end of summer, the children would not let them go back to the farm. She knew something must be afoot when they made them stay at the house in Mengo for a whole week. When they finally drove them home, there was indeed a surprise waiting for them. They turned off the Namugongo Road at the big mango tree, then made a left turn into her driveway. They drove past the front paddocks and she caught a glimpse of some of her calves. It wasn't until they were almost up to the milking shed, that Rebecca looked up and gasped in disbelief. She didn't recognise her house! The children had completely transformed it: the house had been painted; there were rows of flat bricks lining the outside walls and the adjoining kitchen. Inside, there was a new indoor, flushing toilet, the bathroom had been completely renovated and tiled, the bedrooms and sitting room were completely tiled and she had brand new sitting room furniture! Rebecca was overcome with emotion. She said, "Latimer, look what the children have done for us!" It was a lovely homecoming and well worth the wait.

In the middle of 2007, the whole family were gathering to celebrate Rebecca's 75th birthday. They were calling it the 'Mama bash' and it was going to be held in Mombasa, Kenya. Every two years, when grandson Jeremiah came to visit his mother, they would take all the grandchildren on a trip: one year to Bulago on the Ssese Islands; another year to Mweya Safari Lodge in Queen Elizabeth National Park (where they had taken the children thirty years earlier); another year to Mombasa. Although her birthday had already passed, Rebecca's children, their spouses and the grandchildren were gathering from all over the world to celebrate her life! She and her sister Damallie flew down together while some family members went down by bus and train. By this time, Rebecca was no longer as nimble as she had been twenty years earlier when she regularly took the bus down to Nairobi. She had developed a touch of arthritis in her knees and back, and the children wouldn't let her take those long journeys by road or train anymore.

At the beach, each family had its own little cottage, but they were together for every outing and every meal at the hotel. They toured Mombasa, visiting Fort Jesus and the zoo, where the children were delighted to see a one hundred-year-old tortoise and feed the giraffes from their hands. There were lazy afternoons walking on the beach or lounging by the pool. In the evenings, they all got together and joined in the hotel festivities: there were cultural dance performances; there was a karaoke singing contest that was won by Philippa and Bessie; there was a surprise cake for Louise on her birthday; and there was a special tree planting ceremony for Rebecca organised by the hotel. The children gave Rebecca a special 75th birthday card with a message from each family thanking her for being there for them. This always brought tears to Rebecca's eyes. She could only give the thanks back to God who had been her companion and her guide.

One day, they hired a boat and struck out on the Indian Ocean. The captain of the boat made sure everyone ate breakfast, in case they got seasick. The grandchildren were looking forward to snorkelling. At first, the waters were calm and they were able to admire the architecture and variegated colours of the coral reef below. Then they motored out to deeper waters and were surprised when, all of a sudden, there were several dolphins cheekily playing around the boat. The waters were choppy now and some of the family were staying active throwing up over the side of the boat. Several hundred metres out into the ocean, the captain dropped the anchor. The grandchildren suited up with their uncles and slipped into the ocean to start snorkelling. It came naturally to the young ones, but their uncles struggled a bit. Their aunts took the safe option and stayed in the boat. Rebecca had no intention of getting seasick and stayed in her seat too. It was so much fun sitting in the boat chatting with her daughters and watching the grandchildren play in the very Indian Ocean she had sailed when she was just a single girl! They were all quite ready for lunch by the time they came ashore. That was a week to remember!

Later that year, everyone in Kampala watched the news anxiously as riots followed the Kenyan presidential elections of December 2007 and civil war almost broke out. Kenya had always been one of their most stable neighbours and sheltered many a displaced Ugandan. No one wanted to see a repeat of the kind of genocide that had broken out in Rwanda in the mid-1990s. More importantly, Becky and her husband, Fred, were in the process of moving their family to Nairobi. She had been promoted to a new position in her company and had to be relocated. When things did finally settle down, they were able to make the move and the children started school that January.

Back home in Kampala, Rebecca kept herself busy. She designed and started construction on a recreation centre in memory of her parents, Kupliano and Damali Bisase Kisosonkole. After that project, she embarked on building rental houses at Mengo for her sister. She had to sell off more land in order to finish these projects, but it was well worth it. When she completed the rental units, she organised a small thanksgiving service with family members and friends. She was ever grateful to God for every one of her accomplishments.

Rebecca also made regular visits to the Kasubi Tombs to visit the 'concubines' who kept the grounds and took them gifts and food. The new Katikkiro, Honourable J.B. Walusimbi, proved to be very supportive of Rebecca and made sure she had a small stipend to help her fulfil her duties. Her brother, Myers, was supportive in another way: he would ring her at 4 a.m. every morning so that they could pray together with others. Rising early in the morning had always been easy for Rebecca. When she was at home, she attended the 7 a.m. Sunday service at her local parish church, Kamuli. When she was in town, she would attend the 7 a.m. service at Namirembe Cathedral.

Rebecca started regularly attending Bible Study Fellowship (BSF) at the Kampala Baptist Church and made several good friends in the fellowship. When it was in session, BSF became the highlight of her week. She appreciated the opportunity to study the Bible with women from other churches and to meditate on God's Word. She really enjoyed the study of Moses. Rebecca and her daughter Damallie discussed the question of why God did not allow Moses to enter the Promised Land.

Rebecca said, "Moses' work was done. Maybe the Israelites would have turned to worshipping him instead of God if he had entered the Promised Land."

"Mum, *that* is a deep thought," her daughter responded.

As Rebecca had done with her mother when she was young, she made it her duty to check on the ill at home or in hospital. She looked for different ways to provide assistance to those in need where she could. Once she read about a lady in the daily newspaper who had delivered triplets and been abandoned by her husband. She noted the area where she lived and went to look for her. She and her driver found the Local Council Chairman of the area and he directed them to the new mother's house. She took some baby clothes and money for her to buy milk. Rebecca felt truly blessed when she saw the mother's joy. On another occasion, she went to the church at Namirembe Cathedral and asked the assistant Bishop to deliver what she had brought to a woman whose need had been made known during the church service. She always tried to help parents who had problems raising school fees, and she provided desks for the children at a nearby nursery school. It was her way of thanking God for all that He had done for her.

Rebecca was also grateful that God protected her each day that she spent in her house alone. The children had installed an alarm system for her, but she never had to activate it. The only time her house was broken into, she was not there. She had spent the night at her daughter Philippa's house in Mengo. The intruder broke into her bedroom by cutting through the burglar proofing. The only thing that was taken was a bag in which she had put some money she had received that morning, so she was sure it must have been an inside job. Some of the staff on the farm were picked up by the police for questioning, but there was no evidence against them, so she let it go, thanking God for her safety. Some wondered why Rebecca never built herself a large house with an imposing wall and a gate with an armed guard. She didn't want to evoke more people to jealousy and believed that only the Lord could protect her, anyway. Rebecca also lost a sizeable amount of money from her bank account through Automated Teller Machine (ATM) fraud, but even though she reported it, the issue was never resolved and she let that go as well. She was thankful that she still had her life, and that God had been faithful in providing for her.

Chapter Twenty-Nine

Infirmity

Rebecca was now a vibrant member of the 21st century. She still drove herself around the village to visit family and friends, but she absolutely refused to buy an automatic car. When the family wouldn't stop badgering her about it, she finally confessed that she was sure she would fall asleep at the wheel of an automatic car. The arthritis in her legs and back were making it difficult for her to drive in the city. She now had a driver. Her children had coined the term 'tezing' (after her aunt Hannah) to refer to someone who was always on the move. They would tease her that she was always 'tezing' or gallivanting and that's why she needed a driver. Driving in the city had also become quite precarious. While driving in Kampala, not only did you have to avoid other cars, there were numerous taxis and boda-bodas (motorcycles) aggressively weaving in and out of the traffic; there were bicycles, pedestrians and cows and goats to avoid; and if you didn't pay close enough attention, you would land in one of the numerous potholes.

She had resisted for a while, but Rebecca now owned a mobile phone and a laptop computer. She regularly spoke to the children and grandchildren over Skype. In February 2009, Rebecca travelled to Nairobi for a medical check-up. The arthritic pain in her back and knees was becoming a daily reminder of her age. Her grandchildren were as delighted to see her as she was to see them. The doctor treated her arthritis with injections in both knees and prescribed a regimen of specific exercises for her to do. She began following her exercise regimen diligently and continued it when she returned home to Kampala. She was just in time to join the celebrations of the Kabaka's birthday on April 13th: a church service followed by a dinner at the Mengo Palace. Rebecca had kingdom functions to attend, multiple weddings and funerals of relatives and recurring issues involving her land. She had picked out four small plots of land to bequeath to her oldest grandchild, only to discover that one of them had already been sold right under her nose. Then it was reported to her that some relatives were cultivating vegetables on the edge of her property without permission. Was there any honesty left in the land?

The children encouraged Rebecca to start writing her memoirs. It wasn't difficult for her to bring back the memories of life with Mummy and Daddy and Latimer. She began speaking into her tape recorder and writing in her diary. Early one morning in March 2010, Rebecca received some catastrophic news. The Kasubi Tombs had burned to the ground! Not only had an important part of their history been lost in the flames, but also a recognised UNESCO World Heritage site. The President, the Kabaka and the Nnabagereka all toured the site a week later, the Kabaka with tears in his eyes. Riots that broke out among the people were quickly quelled by government security forces. Rebecca felt a deep sense of sadness come over her. It reminded her of the year 1992 that Queen Elizabeth had described as her *'annus horribilis'* when part of the Windsor Castle in England burned down, and her family appeared to be falling apart.

Rebecca waited for a few more days until the rioting had died down. When she did visit the site at Kasubi that had become so familiar to her from her numerous visits, she was shocked by the extent of the damage. All that remained was the charred outline of the beautiful straw thatched dome, built in 1881, that had once housed historic artefacts and treasures of the kingdom. Thankfully, the remains of the four Kabakas who were buried there were not housed in the part of the structure that burned down. But even if the structure was rebuilt, there were articles that could never be replaced. Rebecca felt that somehow they had let their ancestors down. Would the kingdom survive this insult to her very foundation? She had survived the territorial wars with her neighbours, the invasion of the colonialists, the exile of her kings and the desecration of her institutions. And although she had re-emerged as only a fledgling shadow of her former self, held together by only the loose remnants of a once unbreakable allegiance, to Rebecca she was like a sleeping giant. Somewhere in the wilderness, 'Moses' would one day arise to lead the 'children of Buganda' back to the promised land. A year and a half later, the Kabaka was introducing them to his royal baby son, Semakokiro!

There were many family members present to celebrate each new milestone with Rebecca, but she especially appreciated the presence of her sister, Damallie, at each event. They were almost inseparable now and she couldn't wait for her sister to retire so that they could spend their golden years together. They had lost their eldest brother, Dolphe, early in 2010 and in July, they lost Lady Damali Nnabagereka who had been Kabaka Mutesa's widow. Damallie was not at Rebecca's side that July when the 'Little Kagabi' got married, but she was there in early December when Wilfred got married and brought a precious new daughter-in-law, Anna, into the family. Brother-in-law John Serebe stood in for Latimer. Of all her children, Wilfred was the one who had remained nearby when the others scattered, and Rebecca appreciated all that he had done for her. She had prayed that before she departed this life, God would give him a partner to share his life. Her prayer was answered. It was more than answered. She had always appreciated the love shown to her by all her sons-in-law, and now she was blessed with a daughter-in-law nearby who loved and honoured her, too. Her industriousness somehow reminded Rebecca of her own mother and they got along famously.

Rebecca was fast approaching her 80th birthday, but in her mind, she wasn't a day over fifty. The last thirty years seemed to have rushed by, and if it wasn't for the constant pain in her knees and back, she would have had to remind herself of her real age. The children were suggesting that she have her knees operated on so that she could regain her former agility; but she wasn't quite ready for that. She had never been hospitalised except to have her babies and during that one episode of cerebral malaria. Others who had had knee replacement surgery were quite graphic in their description of the pain they had to endure afterwards.

The children finally convinced Rebecca to have her knees operated on the following year. It was becoming difficult for her to walk even short distances. One day, she had gone to inspect one of her children's newly built properties. After walking painfully from the car to the gate leaning on her cane, she took the first opportunity to sit down. There was no way she was going to make the extra yards to go inside the house. She flew to Nairobi in August 2011 to stay with her daughter, Becky, and see a consultant. Rebecca enjoyed being around her other grandchildren again. They would come home from school and chat with their grandmother before heading off to do their homework. The whole family took a trip to the Samburu National Park. Sitting in the safety of their car, they watched the animals with curiosity and were rewarded when they noticed a giraffe in the process of giving birth. Rebecca's grandchildren were amused to hear her edging the cow on with the words, "Push! Push!" just as she did with her own cows.

The Orthopaedic doctor that daughter Louise retained wanted to operate on Rebecca's right knee first. Although it wasn't giving her as much pain as the left one, the x-ray showed that she had no cartilage left in that knee. Rebecca was anxious about undergoing the very first surgery of her life. Her children prayed with her and they all agreed to follow the doctor's orders. Rebecca's first knee operation went well. Post-operatively, though, Rebecca was disoriented for about twenty-four hours. Hypoxia was suspected but her lungs were fine. She also developed a short-lived case of diabetes caused by post-operative steroids. Then when it was time to start walking, it was noticed that she had foot drop (difficulty lifting the foot), so Rebecca had to start physiotherapy for that. Her grandchildren helped her stay focused on her exercise regimen. In between, well-wishers were ringing from America, from England and especially, from Uganda. Eventually, she was able to take longer and longer walks around the neighbourhood and as usual, she made friends with young and old alike. One young girl she befriended spoke only Arabic, Swahili and a little broken English, but they enjoyed each other's company and were often seen taking their walks together.

Rebecca was fully recovered within two months. By the end of the year, she was back in Kampala. Her sister, Damallie, had not been present during the surgery, but she arrived a few weeks later and helped nurse her sister back to health. Philippa had just returned from Norway after completing her PhD in *'Paediatric HIV-1 infection in Uganda'*. She held a thanksgiving service to honour God and her parents. The function was held at 'Crystal Gardens', the project Rebecca had initiated in honour of her own parents. It was a happy celebration. The recreational gardens looked so beautiful with all the decorations. Traditional music was appropriately played to herald Rebecca's arrival.

Philippa thanked her mother for working so hard to provide for them since their father's death and gave her a special thank-you gift. The new head of the Department of Paediatrics, Dr. Sarah Kiguli, gave tribute to their father, the late Professor

Latimer Kamya Musoke. She reminded them that the Acute Care Ward for children at Mulago Hospital had been dedicated to his memory. Rebecca was given an opportunity to say a word herself and, surrounded by her siblings, in-laws, children, grandchildren and friends, in the very place she had built to honour her parents, she told everyone how grateful she was to God for enabling her to see this day. She also told them how thankful she was to be able to walk pain free and without a walking stick!

Rebecca and Damallie were still in Kampala the following March when the Orthopaedic doctor said he wanted to proceed with the operation on her second knee. Rebecca was nervous about proceeding with another surgery so soon, but the doctor was going to be away starting in April. She consulted the rest of the family and they encouraged Rebecca to go ahead with the surgery. She and Damallie travelled to Nairobi to prepare for her second knee operation that March.

Rebecca had not felt or heard anything during her first operation, but during this one, she could hear the doctors talking. It sounded like the doctor was having more trouble with the left knee. She could even hear the sawing of the instruments, although she couldn't feel the motion. It was quite unnerving as, despite hearing all of that, *she* could not communicate with *them*.

After surgery, the pain in her left knee was excruciating, despite therapeutic doses of pain medicine. Rebecca could not remember feeling this much pain in her right knee, even right after the surgery. In addition to that, the scar didn't appear to be as smooth as the other one and it was starting to itch. Rebecca was referred to the dermatologist, but after examining her leg, he only prescribed a short course of topical steroid cream. The doctor thought the problem would be short-lived and sent her home to continue her recovery at Becky's house. She still had to report to the hospital regularly for her physiotherapy sessions. In between, the family tried to keep her distracted by taking her on drives around Nairobi. She observed the real estate construction projects in the area and remarked that she would someday like to build a housing estate like that. Although she had regularly attended Bible Study Fellowship (BSF) after her first operation, she was less mobile now and couldn't attend the weekly sessions. But she made sure she studied the Bible and completed her lesson assignments.

Eldest daughter Damallie had been posted to work in Rome by the World Food Programme. She paid Rebecca a surprise visit for a few days during her recovery. They sat by the swimming pool snacking and discussing plans for the future. A few weeks later, it was Bessie who paid Rebecca a surprise visit from America. Two months later, Rebecca was well enough to travel to London with her sister.

While they were in London, Rebecca and Damallie received some sad news. Two sisters-in-law had passed away in Uganda: Tempora's wife, Joanita and Myers's wife, Proscovia. Joanita had been sick for a while, but Proscovia's sudden death came as a shock to everyone. She had been so alive; enjoying the festivities of the Thanksgiving service just a few months earlier. Rebecca and Damallie could not fly back from England to attend either funeral, but at least they were together to share the pain of losing more close family members.

Chapter Thirty

Thanksgiving

Slowly, Rebecca's knee was getting better, but the itching of her skin was spreading to other parts of her body. Any change could trigger an outbreak: heat or cold, stress or excitement. She felt like her skin was on fire and she desperately needed to scratch the ugly, red blotches on her skin. Worst of all, was the itchy, brown, desquamative rash on her hands which rendered her unable to be useful to her sister. The only areas of her body that were spared were her face and her feet. It was all that her sister could do to keep her from scratching. Consultation with the doctors where Rebecca had had the surgery, and others where she was now recovering, could not uncover the source of her itching. First she was diagnosed with eczema, then psoriasis; but a biopsy showed only chronic inflammation. There would be temporary relief whenever she was given a course of oral steroids. As soon as the steroids were discontinued, she would relapse. Was it an allergic reaction to something in her environment, something in her diet or something that had been placed in her knees? It was a mystery.

Rebecca and her sister returned to Uganda in November. The nation had just celebrated its jubilee: 50 years since the independence of Uganda from the British colonial government on October 9, 1962. Rebecca was also experiencing a repatriation of her own family. Her daughter, Damallie, was coming home after working for four years in Rome and four years before that in Khartoum; daughter Bessie was coming home after thirty years in America. After Christmas, the whole family travelled to Murchison Falls National Park to celebrate Rebecca's 80th birthday. They stayed at a motel on the way to Masindi, from where they would drive out to sightsee. They visited a Rhino Park and the more adventurous of the group went on the Rhino trail on foot and took pictures close up. One day they drove to the Murchison Falls itself. Rebecca missed getting close to the falls because she couldn't walk that far, but the rest gave her a detailed description of it. That Sunday, they had a family worship service and each person was given an opportunity to say something they were thankful for. Everyone was looking forward to 2013 as the year of new beginnings. The children and grandchildren sang and danced. It was certainly going to be a year of new beginnings for Rebecca: Pauline, the "Little Kagabi" was expecting her first child, Rebecca's first great grandchild.

A month before the baby was due, Rebecca travelled to Nairobi to have her skin condition re-evaluated. She saw the dermatologist who had examined her immediately after her surgery and was prescribed a regimen of tablets and creams to help control the itching. Rebecca was back in Kampala in time to witness the birth of her great grandchild. Unlike her mother, she was not born at home, but delivered safely at Nakasero Hospital. They all gathered in her hospital room to celebrate and take pictures with Baby Julia. Three weeks later, the children, grandchildren and great grandchild were all gathered together at Rebecca's house for Easter. After a hearty lunch, they sat on her front veranda and held one of their usual lively discussions. Sometimes they were philosophical, sometimes theological, sometimes they just reminisced over bygone days. The grandchildren loved to hear the stories of how they had all survived the darkest days in Uganda's history. Sitting on her veranda, looking out over the pastures, listening to her family chattering away, Rebecca could not help but be thankful. Her grandson Philip asked her, "With all your past experiences in life, Jjajja, what would you say about it?"

"Life is what you make it," she replied decisively.

The children recommended that Rebecca return to Nairobi to see her doctors so that her rash could be re-evaluated. It was not responding to the latest prescriptions. She travelled to Nairobi two weeks after Easter. Her daughters, Damallie and Bessie, drove her to the airport and got someone to help her get a wheelchair and check in. As she was checking in she suddenly realised she couldn't remember the address where her daughter Louise lived. She asked the attendant to wheel her to where her daughters were waiting outside the glass walls. Through the glass, using lay sign language, she managed to explain what she needed. Damallie wrote the address on a piece of paper in large letters and she copied it down. They laughed as they waved farewell and she went back to check in.

She spent the first month with Becky's family and then moved to Louise's house so that she could have easier access to her doctors. The condition of her rash was fluctuating from day to day. She wasn't walking around as much, partly because of pain in her back and partly because the neighbourhood wasn't conducive to it. Family and friends would ring frequently, but at first she didn't want to make many phone calls herself and incur roaming charges. Her son, Wilfred, advised her not to worry about the cost; keeping in touch with others was one of Rebecca's favourite activities. In between phone calls, she continued with knitting the sweaters that she regularly donated to the premature babies born at Mulago Hospital. She wished that she had her computer or her tape recorder with her to continue recording her memoirs, but she had left those in Kampala. No one had thought she was going to be away this long.

Rebecca had been away about a month when she had a dream. She dreamt that she was telling God what she wanted; He in turn was telling her what *He* wanted to do for her. She didn't dwell on the dream too much; God had already done so much for her. Later that day, she received a phone call from Wilfred with an announcement: her new daughter-in-law was expecting a baby. It was a long six months away, but another of Rebecca's prayers had been answered! Rebecca was ecstatic! She was already knitting a sweater for her new great grandchild; and now, she began knitting one for the new grandchild expected in December.

Rebecca had another dream a few weeks later. She dreamt that she was back in her house on the farm; the Kabaka came to her house bringing her a cake. She asked him why he had not asked someone else to deliver it for him. He replied that he had to bring it himself. When she awoke, Rebecca prayed for him as she always did for all her children and grandchildren. She wasn't sure what the dream meant; maybe a peace offering because she hadn't been able to attend his birthday celebrations on April 13th. She had had to ring the Katikkiro in advance to convey her apologies. Rebecca made several phone calls that week to her brothers. She wanted them all to get together as soon as she returned to Kampala to discuss some lingering family issues. One of them was to schedule the late Damali Nnabagereka's last funeral rites.

The doctor had put Rebecca on a new medicine, an immunosuppressant called Imuran (used to prevent organ rejection in transplant patients), and changed her diet. She was no longer itching, but she asked her son-in-law, Nabeta, to get an extension on her plane ticket so that the doctor could complete his evaluation. She spent the following weekend at Becky's house for a day of pampering. She had her hair dyed and Becky treated her to a manicure and a pedicure. She watched as her grandson, Daudi, and his friend, Maluki, got ready to go to their high school prom. The next day, son-in-law, Isaac, was visiting from Kampala and brought Rebecca a letter from her daughter, Damallie. She also got a welcome phone call from her sister in London. They could always find so much to talk and laugh about across the miles. Rebecca returned to Louise's house that evening. She was a little short of breath when she walked up the stairs, but maybe it was just 'old age creeping up on her.' Louise scheduled a doctor's appointment for Thursday, the 20th of June.

Rebecca attended the Bible study fellowship at Louise's house that Wednesday. At the end, everyone was asked to present their prayer requests. Rebecca said, "No, I don't have a prayer request. I only have thanksgiving to give to God. He has blessed me more than anyone woman deserves in a lifetime. I can only praise and thank Him." After Bible study, they had supper. Then Rebecca made preparations to go to bed. Before she went to bed, she rang her daughter, Bessie. She didn't pick up the phone but called her mother right back. Bessie was concerned that something might be wrong; Mama didn't usually ring that late. But Rebecca just wanted to know how she and her husband were, and to let them know that she was fine. She had enjoyed the Bible Study, her supper and the fact that she had not had any itching for three whole days! After a few minutes, she said, "Let me let you go back to sleep," and they said goodnight to each other.

The next morning, Louise brought her mother breakfast at 6:00 a.m. as usual and left for work with her husband. Rebecca usually liked to take her bath then, so she got out of bed and made her way to the bathroom. Morning toiletry completed, she walked back to the bedroom and sat on her bed, ready to get dressed for the day. If she had been a singer, she would have sung that morning. As it was, her spirit felt light and her heart full of joy. She had so much to be grateful to God for: she had had loving parents and a loving husband; she had a beloved sister and children who cared for her tirelessly. God had given her the strength to persevere despite every obstacle in her way. Her motto: 'where there is a will, there is a way' was unequivocally true. What more could she ask God for?

Rebecca had often looked back on her life and said, "How can I thank you, Lord? I do thank You whenever I can: sometimes I thank You while sitting on my porch; sometimes I thank You while riding in the car; sometimes I wake up at night and just give thanks. I never finished school, I became a widow while still young, but I managed to work and educate all my children! Those were tough times, but You got us through them." She had few regrets in life and never held a grudge against anyone. She had battled with her brothers for so many years over her desire to fulfil her father's wishes; a battle so reminiscent of history repeating itself, but all was forgiven. As she always told her children: to love, to forgive, to be thankful and to remember were the most precious principles she had learnt in life. Her favourite Bible verse, she told them, was 1 John 4:12 – "No one has ever seen God; but if we love one another, God lives in us, and His love is made complete in us."

∞

Rebecca with Adam, Philippa and cousin
Louise in London (Damallie's house).

Rebecca with Dr. and Mrs. Shannon in Scotland.

Rebecca and Damallie with the author in Maryland, U.S.A.

Rebecca and Damallie with Aunt Kanyike, her
daughter and author's husband in New York.

Rebecca with grandson Jeremiah in Maryland, U.S.A.

Rebecca, Philippa and Bessie at Niagara Falls, Canada.

Namasole Rebecca Zirimbuga with
Katikkiro Ssemwogerere (centre)

Namasole Rebecca Zirimbuga with Kabaka Ronald Mutebi II (2nd right)

Namasole Rebecca Zirimbuga being
welcomed to a kingdom function.

Kabaka Ronald Muwenda Mutebi II greeting
Namasole Rebecca Zirimbuga.

Namasole with Nnabagereka Sylvia Nagginda
and Princess Sangalyambogo

Namasole Rebecca Zirimbuga, her sister
and Prince Richard Semakokiro.

Damallie, Philippa and Namasole Rebecca at
the Mama Bash in Mombasa, Kenya.

Namasole Rebecca, Damallie and Philippa.
Thanksgiving service at 'Crystal Gardens'.

Namasole Rebecca Zirimbuga with her family on her 80th birthday. Masindi. 2012

Epilogue

Rebecca had never wanted to suffer a prolonged, debilitating illness that would have left her a vegetable, dependent upon others or on machines for every life-sustaining activity. God granted her wish. She died of a massive pulmonary embolus following deep vein thrombosis; a blood clot that travels from your leg to your lungs and instantly blocks the main artery, preventing oxygen from reaching the bloodstream and blood flowing back to the heart. One moment she was in this world, the next moment she was being welcomed into the next by her Lord and her loved ones who had gone before her. She was ready to cast her crown of righteousness at Jesus' feet. She was free to enter the joy of the Lord who had been her faithful companion and answered her fervent prayers; free to bask in the eternal glow of her Lord's love; free from pain and worry, sorrow and regret; free to run and explore heaven to her adventurous heart's delight, no longer hampered by sore knees, weariness or unanswered questions. She had so much to tell Latimer and Mummy and Daddy about the children, grandchildren and great-grandchildren she had left behind. Rebecca is at peace, knowing that God will faithfully take care of them ... as He had taken care of her since she was a little girl, holding on to her father's firm, guiding hand.

∞

Rebecca was found collapsed on her bed at 8:30 am. An ambulance was called to take her to hospital. All efforts to resuscitate her were futile and she was pronounced dead that Thursday morning, the 20th of June, 2013. Her body was transported from Nairobi to Entebbe by air on Saturday morning. Her family in Nairobi accompanied her and they were met by all the family from Kampala. The body was transported from Entebbe to the mortuary at Mulago Hospital where her family were able to view it. Her daughters were struck by how beautiful and peaceful she looked. The family in England arrived the following day and went to Mulago to view her body as well. The family had wanted to bury her on Monday, but the Buganda government intervened. They advised them that the Namasole could not be buried in obscurity: her passing had to be officially announced in the lukiiko on Monday morning, followed by the funeral service at Namirembe Cathedral in the afternoon.

The funeral service was conducted by her long-time friend, retired Archbishop Emeritus Livingstone Mpalanyi Nkoyoyo. It was attended by the Nnabagereka and the new Katikkiro of Buganda, Peter Mayiga, as well as overflowing crowds of mourners. There was a message from Kabaka Ronald Muwenda Mutebi II, and another from President Yoweri Museveni expressing their condolences and giving financial support. There were dignitaries from the Buganda government and the central government of Uganda in attendance, as well as family and close friends from all walks of life.

The funeral service was organised by the children's cousin, Grace Sengaaga, and emceed by the son of Latimer's long-time friend, Herbert Semambo. All who eulogised Rebecca and laid wreaths paid tribute to her hardworking spirit, her integrity and sense of duty, her perpetual orientation towards people, her unending love for her family, her spirit of adventure and her firm faith in God. She had put all her affairs in order, including her will, in which she had named her successor, and expressed her wish for a closed casket and desire to be buried next to her husband in Makonzi, Ssingo. Tradition would have required that, as Namasole, she be buried at her unfinished 'palace' in Bumbu, but the Buganda government granted her final wish and allowed her to be buried in the place of her choosing.

The following day, after the heir had been properly installed, Rebecca was transported to her final resting place in Makonzi. She was laid to rest next to Latimer, at the feet of his mother and her father-in-law. Five days after her funeral, Rebecca's family travelled back to Makonzi to pay their respects privately. The wreaths that had been placed over her gravesite were still fresh as they gathered around it and thanked God for her life. After lunch, they were sitting in their cousin John Masembe's sitting room discussing the events of the past few days when the ground began to shake. It was just a tremor, not violent enough to alarm anyone but lasting long enough to be felt by all who were present. A few days later, they were back in Kampala when there was another tremor; this one more significant but still not violent enough to cause any damage to property or loss of life. It was nothing compared to the earthquake of 1966, but some couldn't help wondering.... was Rebecca admonishing them never to forget the land of the kingdom?

Rebecca took with her great pearls of wisdom that she had garnered throughout her eighty-one years. She had managed to successfully navigate the changing times; from her childhood in the era of colonialism; through the glory days of the kingdom and the ugly period of political unrest and terror – to see her family grow and thrive, despite the heartbreaks. One of her greatest achievements was to guide and deliver the restoration of the cultural monarchy without taking on a prominent and possibly divisive role. She played a political role without being a politician and for that, her true contribution will never be widely appreciated, but that in no way diminishes what she achieved.

Rebecca's worth may not have been recognised as much in life as in death; but, the little girl who had grown up wanting nothing more than to be a faithful wife and mother was given a state funeral at the nation's largest cathedral. Her children pondered over what would be the most fitting tribute to her remarkable life. Rebecca's headstone reads: *"I have fought the good fight, I have finished the race, I have kept the faith."* 2 Timothy 4:7

NAMASOLE
REBECCA ZIRIMBUGA MUSOKE
19.02.1932 20.06.2013
"NNWANYE OKULWANA
OKULUNGI, OLUGENDO
NDUTUUSIZZA, OKUKKIRIZA
NKUKUUMYE"

Afterword

The Minister for Culture and Tradition in his own words:

I am Omutaka Kayiira Gajuule Kasibante Fredrick David (Head of the Buffalo Clan). I first met Namasole Rebecca Zirimbuga in the year 1993 (the year of restoration of the Buganda Kingdom). My late aunt, Rosalio Kyoteka Mukudde, officially introduced us and told me, "This is the Kabaka's mother!" I started noting her presence at various kingdom functions but was afraid to approach her because of her exalted status. After Ssabasajja Kabaka had appointed me as Minister of Culture and Tradition, I began to approach Owekitiibwa (Honourable) Namasole Zirimbuga, especially when the Ssabasajja Kabaka began preparing to introduce the Nnabagereka of Buganda to his people.

One thing I observed of Rebecca Zirimbuga in her role as Namasole is that she took her motherly role very seriously and frequently tried to give her royal son advice. On difficult matters that arose concerning the kingdom, Owekitiibwa Namasole would not sleep; she would come to me saying, 'What should we do? What is the best thing to be done in this situation?' She frequently attempted to go to the palace to meet with the Kabaka to discuss issues, but unfortunately, the gatekeepers did not appreciate her value and would often turn her away without informing him. Times had certainly changed since those of our forefathers when the Namasole held such a crucial role in the kingdom!

The second thing I noted about her, was how much she valued your friendship when she trusted you. She became like a parent to me and treated me like her son, often entrusting me with responsibilities beyond the scope of our designated relationship. During this time, I determined that one of the most important things I could do would be to locate or build an official residence for the Namasole, the mother of the kingdom.

I approached the reigning Katikkiro (Prime Minister), Owekitiibwa (Honourable) Joseph Mulwanyammuli Ssemwogerere, to discuss the matter. Many of those present insisted that her official palace should be the one located at Lusakka of Lukuli in Makindye, Kyadondo County, Kampala. However, at that time it was being occupied by the Namasole of Kabaka Mutesa II and she could not be displaced. I suggested to the Katikkiro that he approach the Kabaka to grant us another piece of land, within the kingdom, on which a new palace could be built.

I was granted authority by Ssabasajja Kabaka to approach the Buganda Land Board. We began searching for an appropriate piece of land. We found some land in Konge and we were ready to purchase it but, on closer examination, I decided it was too small for the Namasole as it only amounted to 20 decimals. The Katikkiro and I went back to the Kabaka and petitioned for a larger piece of land of 2 or 3 acres from his own personal land that would be fitting for the mother of the king.

Ssabasajja Kabaka agreed and I embarked on a new search. I found land in a place called Bumbu, which is located on the road to Gayaza via Kitangobwa, Buwambo Road. I immediately went and picked up Mama Namasole and brought her and all those who were with her to the place. I said, 'This is it!' and we surveyed the land together. Thankfully, she approved of it and gave permission for us to begin building her palace.

∞

The Kabaka's wedding preparations were now in full gear. We had to start and finish the new palace in time for Mama Namasole to perform her official duties prior to the wedding of the Kabaka to his Nnabegereka. I approached the Minister of Finance, Owekitiibwa (Honourable) J.B. Walusimbi and requested for financial assistance in building the Namasole's palace. He understood the need, but replied that because of the limited financial resources of the kingdom, he did not know where they could find any extra money for this task. He suggested that they might have to take some money out of that which would be collected for the wedding, but only as a last resort.

We received some money from the Buganda Land Board to begin buying building materials, but the bulk of the money for her hastily built palace had to be provided by Namasole Zirimbuga herself, the first Namasole to build her own palace. Before we could begin building the palace, we had to get official blessing from the leaders of various clans: from the Mbogo (Buffalo) clan, from the Mbwa (Dog) clan, from the Engo (Leopard) clan and from Mugema, leader of the Nkima (Monkey) clan. As you know, these processes take time.

The building had not gone very far, when they suddenly announced the date of the Kabaka's wedding on August 27th, 1999. Mama Namasole had to perform the ceremony of sending off her son into holy matrimony in this shell of a building. But she performed the rituals well and the rest of the ceremonies proceeded accordingly.

∞

Namasole Zirimbuga used to confide in me some of the things that troubled her:

The role of Namasole was no longer respected as it had once been and she was often not recognised. She wondered whether the late Sarah Kabejja could have fulfilled the role better. I responded that we would never know, as she was no longer with us, but it probably would have been just as difficult. 'No one gets to choose their mother', I said, 'But it is you who has been granted the responsibility during this critical time by those who entrusted it to you.' I am thankful to God that He heard my prayers and that Namasole Zirimbuga continued in her role until her untimely departure from this world.

Another thing that made things difficult for us was that we were being given advice by so many different people on how to fulfil our roles as bearers of the torch of maintaining the culture and traditions of Buganda. We had financial constraints; transportation was difficult, especially as we often had to travel at night. After each function, I had to make sure the Namasole and the Katikkiro had transport back to their homes before I could return to mine. People often asked me why I cared so much about her safety; she was the Kabaka's mother, not mine. But I didn't care what they said; I knew it was my responsibility to take care of her.

Truthfully, the unity that we had going through those difficult times is what helped us to re-establish the kingdom in those early years. The current Namasole should be grateful for all that Mama Namasole Zirimbuga endured in her efforts to support the newly restored kingdom. There were things that were painful for her to do, but if they fostered the restoration of the Kingdom of Buganda, she was willing to knuckle down and do them. As you know, she was a woman of faith, but that did not stop her from meeting the challenges that were demanded by her role.

I remember another occasion that was difficult for Mama Namasole. We had a ceremony to attend some distance from Kampala. The ceremony was going to be held at night during the national election season, so we knew there would be numerous roadblocks along the way. We sat down to figure out what we were going to do. The leaders in the lukiiko (parliament) had assured us this was one event we needed to attend. We did not want to delay in fulfilling any instructions we were given.

When we got into the car, I was going to drive. Then I told Mama Namasole, 'No, you drive. It will be easier for us at the roadblocks when they see a distinguished elderly lady driving, rather than a young man.' She agreed and we were able to get through the roadblocks without incidence. To both our horror, when we got there, there had already been a carnal, ritual sacrifice performed. Neither of us had ever seen anything like it and we never spoke of it again.

Transport to functions such as these had to be arranged privately because we were not allowed to use official vehicles. Neither did we want to use our own cars by which people would have been able to identify us. We had to hire taxis, but there was no money provided for us to attend these functions – none at all! We probably visited every single county in Buganda in search of our history. We crossed streams, we crossed rivers, we crossed lakes. It was like clearing a path through a formidable jungle.

What Namasole Rebecca Zirimbuga did can never be matched. She slept in the bush; she slept in the cold; she would go all day without a meal; sometimes all we had to drink was water. She did all this for her royal son and the Kingdom of Buganda. When Namasole became ill, I was concerned that we would no longer be able to fulfil our responsibilities. Then she would often send me alone, but would provide her car for me to use when I had to travel to remote places. That was our responsibility: to make sure the kingdom was re-established.

∞

What was it that Buganda needed? First, it had to be verified that each function we performed would be beneficial to the rebuilding of the kingdom. Secondly, we needed to be granted the authority to perform the functions on behalf of the Kabaka. Many people may not have understood that what we were doing was on behalf of the kingdom. However, we did not carry out our responsibilities on our own behalf, but as representatives of the kingdom.

How did we accomplish this purpose? First of all, we had singleness of purpose. If we met an obstacle, it helped *that there were three or four of us in agreement: myself, Owekitiibwa Katikkiro Mulwannyamuli Ssemwogerere, Owekitiibwa Namasole Zirimbuga and our leader, Ssabasajja Kabaka Muwenda Mutebi II. Even when he was not with us, we knew we had his authority and blessing in our endeavours. I am grateful to Namasole Zirimbuga that in all that we accomplished together, she never turned around and broadcast it to others, not even her children. I believe this is one of the reasons we were able to achieve success.*

I am also grateful to Owekitiibwa Namasole for her fortitude. At her age and health, coupled with all the work she did, I often thought she would give up some of her duties; but she didn't. She loved Buganda and she loved people. There wasn't a 'concubine' or an aide in any of the outlying palaces or royal tombs who didn't know who she was. She would send them encouragement through me telling them to be strong and support the kingdom, support the Kabaka; because if the kingdom failed, it would be detrimental to us all.

Her courage and determination were often demonstrated in our endeavours, even when I myself did not feel as confident. Like the time when she was turned away at the Kabaka's palace gates. I thought the disappointment might make her give it all up; but she persevered and taught me to continue serving my master with or without acknowledgement. She loved the clan elders and many of them became her friends. She chatted freely with them and would also ask them for advice.

She did her own research and would not perform a function without researching it first. She would ask advice from the Katikkiro, from one elder and another; so that by the time you sat down to discuss it, she could give you a summary of the different recommendations she had received. By that means, we came to a consensus and were able to satisfy the requirements of each responsibility. We were never found to be in error, not because we had vast experience, but because we did a lot of research.

∞

Regarding the verification of the Kabaka's Omulongo ("Ritual Twin"), I will not say much. It was one of the most important things we did; to locate and confirm the identity of the Kabaka's Omulongo. This endeavour required several trips to various locations, sometimes with her brothers, sometimes with the Katikkiro. She needed help to fulfil her responsibilities and I felt it was my duty to assist her, especially in this crucial matter.

We strove to and were fortunate to complete this function required of the Namasole of Buganda, without which she could not be satisfied as having fulfilled her duty as the Mother of Buganda. Afterwards, we had to go to Kasubi where the Namasole catered a large banquet. From there we went to Kajaga where she spent several days catering more days of feasting. After that, we reported to Ssabasajja Kabaka and were received with much ceremonial rejoicing.

One thing I have not talked about that was difficult for Mama Namasole (and she'll forgive me for bringing it up) is that when we began our journey she was still using her married name: Rebecca Kamya Musoke. I asked her if she would be willing to give it up in favour of the name that we had chosen instead. At first, she refused and I had to use clout and tell her that it was Owekitiibwa Mulwanyammuli's wish that she use the name of Zirimbuga, given by her grandmother at birth, as more befitting of her status. She eventually gave in and that became the name associated with her official title until her death.

Throughout her tenure as the Namasole, the one thing that hurt Mama most was the time when the Nnalinyas claimed that Ssabasajja was not the son of his father, nor the rightful heir to the throne! The next day, Mama Namasole got up early; she didn't eat breakfast or lunch and came to me saying, 'What are we going to do about this matter?' That's when I saw how much she loved her royal son; a mother is always a mother. Whatever befalls him is painful to her.

I myself was at a loss for what to say or do. Thankfully, those who had taken over the Kasubi Tombs came to their senses and the situation died down. We both breathed a sigh of relief. But from that time, I could tell that the incident had deeply wounded her. She kept asking, 'How could anyone question that after so many years?' 'Had they lost their minds?' I think it was a good thing that we kept quiet and did not dignify their claims by any response that would have given them credence.

Today, honour is not given to those to whom it is due. The protocol must be reestablished, starting with the Ssabasajja Kabaka, then Namasole, Lubuga, other princes and princesses, clan leaders etc. Some serving in the kingdom are taking the honour for themselves, even though they are only servants. Those I have mentioned serve as owners, not hirelings and should be honoured as such. They are the pillars of the kingdom, and I believe that one day, protocol will be restored just as the kingdom was restored.

Omutaka Kayiira Gajuule

Acknowledgements

I, Elizabeth Musoke Mubiru, would like to acknowledge my profound indebtedness to my siblings in the authorship of this book. I know that bringing back the memories of our mother has not been easy, but I hope that it has been as therapeutic for you all as it has been for me.

Thank you, Adam Musoke, for your consistent counsel and all the anecdotes from our childhood. Thank you, Damallie Kasana, for your excellent memories, editing skills and wise counsel. Thank you, Louise Lwai-Lume, for being my very first editor and for being our persistent prayer warrior. Thank you, Philippa Musoke, for suggesting that I take up the mantle of Mama's memoirs and for coining the title. Thank you, Wilfred Musoke, for being the family historian and coming up with juicy bits of information. Thank you, Becky Lwebuga Kaggwa, for being our financial adviser and keeping me grounded.

A special thank you to our favourite Auntie Damallie Kisosonkole; for loving and caring for our mother, your sister, in such a special way. This book would not have been possible without your detailed diaries, your tenacious interviews and your inspiring support. Thank you to my brothers and sisters-in-law; to all my nieces and nephews, especially Philip Matovu and Pauline Mutumba, for your technical skills and legal counsel.

A special thank you, also, to the Honourable J.G. Mulwanyammuli Ssemwogerere and the Honourable Kayiira Gajuule, both of whom took time out of their busy schedules to lend their expertise and support to this project. Thank you to my final editors, Christine Semambo Sempebwa; Beatrice Langa and Eve Ojok, my lifelong friends. Thank you also to Dr. and Mrs. David and Dorothy Shannon for their detailed, complimentary review of the book. Thank you to all of those who took the time to pen their memories of the unforgettable lady we call, "Maama".

I am grateful to you Maama (Mum) and Taata (Dad) for all the sacrifices you made to pour such a rich inheritance into us, academically and personally, which has made me what I am today. Thank you also to the Jjajjas (our grandparents), 'Afuka Chai' and 'Avuga Landrova' who made our childhood so special. And thank you to the Kabali and Kamanyi families who stepped in to help Maama when our father passed away.

Thank you to many others who supported me along the way: Alan Pritchard at Nakasero Primary School, who first recognised my literary desires; Sheelagh Warren at Gayaza High School, who encouraged me to search for truth; Pamela Daniels at Wellesley College, who eased my transition into American life; Tami Fisk and Helen Roberts without whose assistance I would never have made it through medical school.

Last, but certainly not least, thank you to my husband, Charles Mubiru, for always being there for me. My utmost praise, however, I reserve for the Lord Jesus Christ, whose inspiration and anointing has enabled me to do far more than I could ever think or imagine – from the cleft of the Rock of Ages.

Appendix A

Rebecca's Motto

LOVE, FORGIVE, REMEMBER and BE THANKFUL

"He giveth more grace as our burdens grow greater, He sendeth more strength as our labors increase; To added afflictions He addeth His mercy, To multiplied trials He multiplies peace.

His love has no limits, His grace has no measure, His power no boundary known unto men; For out of His infinite riches in Jesus; He giveth, and giveth, and giveth again.

When we have exhausted our store of endurance, When our strength has failed ere the day is half done, When we reach the end of our hoarded resources; Our Father's full giving is only begun.

Fear not that thy need shall exceed His provision, Our God ever yearns His resources to share; Lean hard on the arm everlasting, availing; The Father both thee and thy load will upbear."

By Annie Johnson Flint

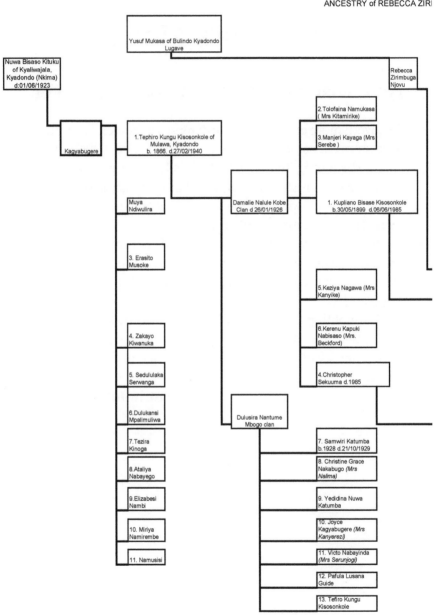

Yusuf Mukasa of Bulindo Kyadondo Lugave

Nuwa Bisaso Kituku of Kyaliwajala, Kyadondo (Nkima) d:01/06/1923

Rebecca Zirimbuga Njovu

Kagyabugere

1.Tephiro Kungu Kisosonkole of Mulawa, Kyadondo b. 1866. d.27/02/1940

2.Tolofaina Namukasa (Mrs Kitamirike)

3.Manjeri Kayaga (Mrs Serebe)

Muya Ndiwulira

Damalie Nalule Kobe Clan d 26/01/1926

1. Kupliano Bisase Kisosonkole b.30/05/1899 d.06/06/1985

3. Erasito Musoke

5.Keziya Nagawa (Mrs Kanyike)

4. Zakayo Kiwanuka

6.Kerenu Kapuki Nabisaso (Mrs. Beckford)

5. Sedululaka Serwanga

4.Christopher Sekuuma d.1985

6.Dulukansi Mpalimuliwa

Dulusira Nantume Mbogo clan

7.Tezira Kinoga

7. Samwiri Katumba b.1928 d.21/10/1929

8.Ataliya Nabayego

8. Christine Grace Nakabugo (Mrs Nalima)

9.Elizabesi Nambi

9. Yedidina Nuwa Katumba

10. Miriya Namirembe

10. Joyce Kagyabugere (Mrs Kanyerezi)

11. Namusisi

11. Victo Nabayinda (Mrs Serunjogi)

12. Pafula Lusana Guide

13. Tefiro Kungu Kisosonkole

Appendix B

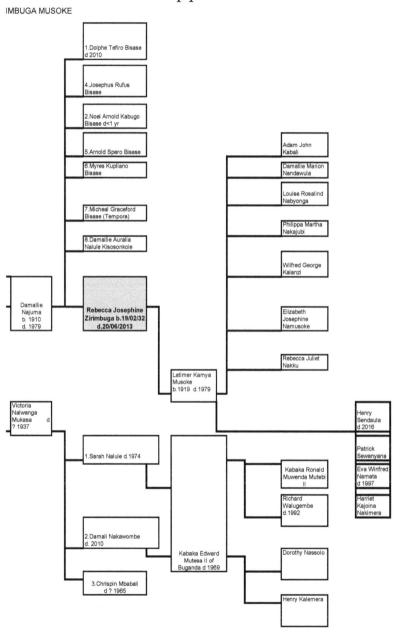

Courtesy: W.G.K. Musoke

Appendix C

Map of Kampala

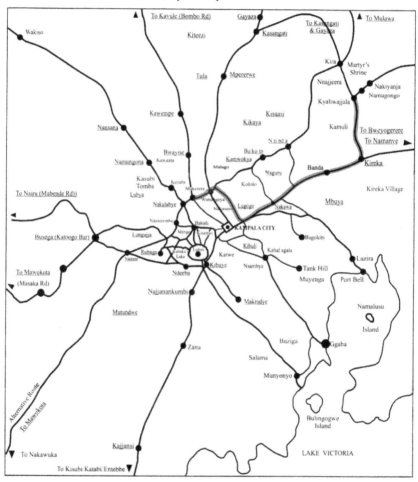

Courtesy: Dr. A.S. Bisase

Glossary

Abaana	Children
Baganda	The people of the Kingdom
Boda-boda	Motorcycle taxi
Buganda	The Kingdom
Bulange	The Parliament building
Busulu	Property taxes
Busuti	Woman's traditional dress
Gombolola	Sub county
Jjajja	Grandparent
Kabalagala	Pancakes
Kabaka	King of Buganda
Kagabi	Water buck
Katikkiro	Prime Minister of Buganda
Kawuna	Tag
Kawunga	Maize meal
Kitiibwa	Honour
Kojja	Maternal uncle
Lubiri	Palace
Lubuga	King's special sister
Lubugo	Bark cloth
Luganda	The language of the people
Lukiiko	Parliament of Buganda
Lumbe	Funeral wake
Mubala	Drumbeat
Mabugo	Donations at a funeral

Malaya	Prostitute
Matoke	Plantains
Mugema	Head of the monkey clan
Mulangira	Prince
Mulongo	Twin or umbilical cord
Muluka	Parish
Mumbejja	Princess
Mutaka	Clan elder
Nabikande	Royal midwife
Namasole	Queen mother
Nnabagereka	Queen
Nnalinya	King's sister
Nnyabo	Madam
Ssabaganzi	King's maternal uncle
Ssabasajja	Man above men
Ssaza	County
Ssebo	Sir
Ssekabaka	Late King
Ssenga	Paternal aunt

References

1. A History of Buganda from the Foundation of the Kingdom to 1900. M.S.M. Semakula Kiwanuka. Longman 1972
2. A Political History of Uganda. S.R. Karugire. Heineman Educational Books 1980
3. "I tried to kill Obote for attacking the Kabaka's palace." Interview of Dan Kamanyi in the *Daily Monitor*. September 15, 2013
4. WAR IN UGANDA: The Legacy of Idi Amin. Tony Avirgan and Martha Honey. Tanzania Publishing House 1982
5. The Screwtape Letters. C.S. Lewis. Geoffrey Bles 1942
6. "The Uganda Agreement of 1900" from Buganda Home Page. Mukasa E. Ssemakula.

Tributes to Namasole Rebecca Zirimbuga Musoke

HEAD OF THE BUFFALO CLAN - MINISTER FOR CULTURE AND TRADITION

The Kisosonkole family has a responsibility to remember the Honourable Rebecca Zirimbuga because of what she did. When she inherited the role of Namasole, there was no Kingdom of Buganda and now there is; there was no prestige associated with the role as there was in the days of Sarah Kabejja, now there is. She served faithfully under the most difficult of circumstances and her family should remember this. Buganda should also remember her because they may not recognise it, but what they see today started with almost nothing. I am grateful for her amazing contributions.

I learnt many things from Mama Namasole:

First, to be strong. Secondly, to work hard. I had many of my own dreams, but after looking at her lifestyle, I began putting my words into action. When it seems like I can't keep on going, I remember how hardworking she was at her age and being so much younger, I keep on working. It was a great lesson for me. Thirdly, she never expressed anger. If she was displeased with you, her displeasure would dissolve quickly. I thought that was a good trait for a leader; not to be bitter. Fourthly, she taught me how to solve problems. Whatever difficult situation we encountered, she persevered and before long, it would be over. Fifthly, she was a good listener; whether someone was being truthful or lying to her, she always listened. Then she would weigh the evidence, weed out the lies and make her own decision how to proceed. I often use this method now in making my own decisions.

On a personal level, my parents celebrated their 50th wedding anniversary and Namasole was the guest of honour. I gave a speech in honour of my parents and she so loved it, she requested a copy for herself. She said that in the 20 years since we met, she had never heard me speak so well. She asked me, jokingly, if the speech was my own or something I had copied from someone else. We were so pleased and honoured that she was able to attend my parents golden wedding anniversary.

Soon after that function, I became very ill and was near death. I cannot forget that Ssabasajja sent Omutaka Mbaziira, head of Nyange (Egret) clan to visit me. Namasole, herself, came to visit me and was so helpful to my family. It was a difficult time and she supported my family through it all. I will never forget that and I always thank God for what she did. I think she remembered and appreciated how I had taken care of her over the years.

By the time she died, Mama Namasole was concerned about those aspects of her role she had been unable to fulfil. I reminded her of the amount of good she *had* done for the kingdom and that no one can do everything. Whatever she was unable to fulfil, the good Lord would raise up others after her to do. They would be able to build on what she had established. Soon after that, she was taken to Nairobi for treatment. She rang me once from there. The next time I tried to ring her, someone told me she was in hospital. The next thing I heard was that the Lord had called her home.

The hardest thing for me is to realise that she did not see much of the fruits of her labour, such as the 20th anniversary of Ssabasajja Kabaka's coronation that we celebrated on July 31st, 2013. It was a glorious celebration which she missed by only two months! The kingdom has developed so much since the struggles of the early days. They have completed the Bumbu palace that was meant for her. She spent one night in it before the royal wedding, but never got to enjoy it as a palace. That should have been hers to enjoy since, in the past, she would have been second in command in the kingdom.

I would like to thank all those who helped the Namasole, especially those who gave her advice regarding her role in the kingdom. Since I was only three years old when the Kabaka's father, Ssekabaka Mutesa II, was deposed and a grown man by the time the kingdom was restored, I could not be of much use in advising her on her role: her responsibilities, how she should behave, how she should be honoured, what her palace should look like and what customs should be performed prior to building her palace. Even though our roles were inherited, we both had to learn on the job. And although we were not able to accomplish everything, we were able to get much of the Namasole role restored. Those who come after her will be able to enjoy the fruit of the hardships she endured.

I would also like to appreciate the efforts of the Honourable Mulwanyammuli Ssemwogerere, Katikkiro at that time, for his contribution to the Office of Culture and Tradition. It is not easy to bring something to birth or rebirth, as in this case, but we did it!

OMUTAKA KAYIIRA GAJUULE

∞

I have known Mama *Namasole* for a very long time. She was a very special, lovely person with a caring attitude towards others. She was such a people person that she cared for rich and poor alike, as well as those not thought of or rated in society. Her caring attitude could be seen in her concern for the Kabaka, as well as for the herdsmen who worked on her farm or any of her projects.

She had a fantastic knowledge base and could converse comfortably on any subject. Despite this and the exalted role that was expected of her, she was humble and never carried herself as if above others. She came from a very important family lineage: her father, Kupliano Bisase, teacher at King's College Budo; her grandfather, ex-Katikkiro Tefiro Kisosonkole;

her husband, Paediatrician and Professor Latimer Musoke... but she was *always* humble.

She always aspired to keep time, especially on important occasions; however, she seemed to be able to create time for others, even if she was supposed to be somewhere else. She displayed sympathy – in fact, empathy towards those less fortunate than she was. She always wanted good things for others.

She loved the Kabaka very much. Whenever she knew or heard something about him, she always wanted to share this information with him and was sometimes frustrated when she could not communicate with him. Her love and care for him was also expressed in the way that whenever she prayed, she prayed for him.

Mama was a good example and the most important things I learnt from her were: forgiveness, kindness, humility and LOVE for all kinds of people.

Honourable Nelson Kawalya
(Speaker of the Parliament)

∞

My sister, Rebecca, may be remembered in her childhood days as a very stubborn young lady over matters of choice; the choice of a certain dress or being forced to eat rice instead of her favourite matoke.

We the younger ones, especially Josephus, would fear the consequences because our father was a very strict disciplinarian. Josephus would rather miss his dinner too; even getting locked outside of our home at night at Budo, to offer companionship to our older sister who refused to eat her rice.

It took me a lifetime to understand that behind that stubbornness and apparent defiance of certain parental instructions, no objection or rebellion was ever intended. In fact, each such apparent impasse was always followed by the most intimate, caring interaction possible between her and our loving parents. Clearly, this was the resoluteness of this young spirit establishing its solid foundation.

If she had not learned early to stand her ground; to make choices, some happy but many difficult ones, what Destiny had in store for her would have broken her will; and with it, her courage and determination to win life's challenges as admirably as she did.

It is sad that Latimer left her so early and with seven offspring to nurture, guide, educate and develop into such dependable beings. Yes, it was sad, but Rebecca's foundation was already there to persevere and finally, decisively, to win. And before the end she shouldered the noble role and duties of Namasole to our King, Ssabasajja Kabaka Ronald Muwenda Mutebi II.

As I look back to those testing times at King's College Budo and reflect on the end results of the enduring love of Latimer and Rebecca, I thank God for a life well lived and with so much grace.

Dr. Arnold Spero Bisase (Brother)

∞

My family, friends and acquaintances of the late Rebecca Musoke Zirimbuga, please agree with me that it is very difficult to write about her life.

Personally, I called her 'Maama' because she was truly like a mother to me, although I should have called her 'Baaba' because she was my older sister. Based on the love, friendship and support she gave me, she was like a parent to me, as if I was one of her children.

Namasole Rebecca helped so many people especially with regards to the Kingdom of Buganda. As one of the children of Damali and Kupliano Bisase, I must say that we were very well loved by our parents. Mrs Rebecca Musoke, as I sometimes called her, continued this special love towards us, her siblings. She helped me to educate my children.

She was designated the administrator of our father's estate when he passed away and she carried out her duties faithfully, transferring to each of us our land titles without a fuss. While she was administrator, she did not indiscriminately sell or give away the land.

To the family, I must say, we should honour Mrs. Musoke for all that she did in representing us so well everywhere she went. We should also never forget how well she looked after our parents before they passed away. On behalf of my brothers and sister, I am grateful for all that she did for us in this life. I am also grateful to her children for continuing her legacy and getting along with us.

Another thing I cannot forget is that because of Mrs. Musoke, the name of KISOSONKOLE is still renowned. She was able to do this because of how well she behaved towards other people and how she fulfilled her role of Namasole of Buganda.

There are so many good things that our sister wanted for us, especially that we should remain united and be able to work together; the same values that our parents tried to instil in us before they left this world.

I pray to God that He will let my sister rest in eternal peace and reward her for all the good she did for others.

Myers Bisase (Brother)

∞

My daughter Rebecca Musoke Namasole Zirimbuga was a loving person. She never discriminated against anyone whether rich or poor, member of the royalty or commoner. But the thing that impressed me most about her is how much she appreciated family. She was always visiting members of her extended family, no matter how far away it was or what the place looked like – she would reach you. No matter what condition or station of life you were in, she loved you. Where else can you find such a person?

May the Lord forgive her for any wrongs and may He let her soul rest in peace. May she rest in the bosom of Jesus for ever and ever! Amen.

Maama Eva Njuki (heir to Rebecca's mother)

∞

I am not going to call her Rebecca, but simply Becca, because that is how her Mum and Dad addressed her. How do I know? I was there.

Becca excelled in her belief as regards family; in fact, I'll call it 'familyhood' which embraces a wider implication in respect to the Kisosonkoles and far beyond. Even in later years and with serious ailments, Becca felt duty bound to visit – check on the wellbeing of the offspring of her family tree.

In hindsight, we should have recorded the historical events associated with our roots. Indeed, it is true that the three of us discussed it on numerous occasions, but somehow we never got around to it. It was always a pleasure to listen to Becca expounding on the yesterdays by sheer memory.

On the subject of her memory, I have a very old photograph of the Kisosonkoles (*our grandparents*) in my possession with quite a few youngsters sitting alongside. I could not, nor could Damallie, identify any of the youngsters. The elders were identified by their *traditional* robes. The mystery of the youngsters was quickly dispelled by Becca who gave us a land scale lecture on each one. Among the youngsters was my mother!

On behalf of Betty, Nancy, Eddie and Solome, we feel humbled and indeed privileged to share the same grandfather as our late beloved Becca. We miss her.

Duncan Serebe (Cousin)

∞

Jjajja Namasole, why do I call her Jjajja? It is because my paternal grandmother, Miria Ntade Namirembe, was a sister to Tefiro Kisosonkole. That made the Kisosonkole line 'bukojja' to my father Hamu Tamale-Nsubuga. As a Muganda, everyone from that line is a Jjajja to me.

However, my relationship with Jjajja Namasole was deeper than that. She loved me and I loved her, too. She visited me quite often and tried as much as possible not to come empty-handed. She would carry a 5 litre jerry can of milk from her farm, Nabwojjo. This continued until she found out that none of us was really very fond of milk.

When she found out that our daughter had delivered a baby girl, she said she was going to knit a sweater and booties for the baby. I thought she was joking and told her I had a beautiful knitting book. She borrowed it and came back with a beautiful, white baby sweater and booties. And eventually, she brought the knitting book back. That was quite commendable because a lot of people borrow things but do not return them!

I am sure she fulfilled her Namasole duties to the best of her ability, without compromising her Christian faith. One day, she came to my house and said she had something she wanted me to do for her. I said, "Anything." It turned out she wanted me to be a signatory on her will! I was taken aback because to me, a will is not written until one is about to die. I told her she was not going anywhere, why was she talking about it? She said she was getting on in years and didn't have many years left.

From that day, she kept reminding me to go to her lawyer and sign. One day, I went and did as she requested. Less than a year after I signed, she was gone. Lord and Saviour Jesus Christ! I have no doubt she is resting in perfect peace. Her favourite hymn 266 in the centenary hymnal says it all. She trusted Jesus the Lord and Him alone!

Mrs. Ruth Mayanja-Nkangi (Cousin)

∞

Rebecca and I met in 1946 at Kings College, Budo as fresh students in J1 and that began a relationship that grew into more than a friendship; we became sisters. Arnold, Rebecca's brother, later married my little sister Connie. This was one of those relationships that was one of its kind in my lifetime.

Our friendship lasted over 50 years; our husbands Latimer and Nelson were very good friends; we had the privilege of knowing and relating with each other in different seasons of life. We celebrated our weddings on the same date, 12th January, but different years; we started families. Rebecca and Latimer often made space for me and my Nelson in their London home when we lived and studied abroad. We watched the children grow, attended their weddings and have seen the grandchildren. I have also had the joy and privilege of knowing and relating with her siblings, her brothers and her dear sister Damallie.

Rebecca was by my side when my mother and my Nelson were sick and when they died; she often came by and offered great support and comfort through these visits.

People quickly warmed up to Rebecca because she was a cheerful woman, sincere and down to earth. She was very practical in the way she related with people from different walks of life: young, middle aged, old; the rich, middle class and those with challenges felt valued and were therefore drawn to her.

Rebecca was a Christian. It was not just what she said: *She lived it out!* Because we related for so many years, there was always something to learn from her. She was brilliant and a quick thinker with a good command of the English language – you paid attention when she spoke. Rebecca was wise, therefore, I and many others were either on the phone with her or at her door step to seek her wise counsel when we were going through challenging situations. Rebecca was a quick thinker; she was also a quick walker - sometimes you had to run to catch up with her steps.

Rebecca's wisdom was made available to people from different contexts of life. Whatever she learned, she was eager to show someone else and share her knowledge. She did farming, sewed and knitted. Many of her friends picked up the knitting skills from her; I became an expert in knitting like her. She inspired me to make things and finish them. She was very hardworking, especially on her farm and she shared milk with us.

As the eldest girl in the family, she set a great example of loving and living selflessly. She cared for her parents, especially when they were unwell, and took her siblings under her wing.

Rebecca's family was her world. She loved, respected and cared for her husband, Latimer. Rebecca's husband and children never left our conversations. She was overly involved in the details of their lives. They knew they were loved because mummy always offered to be there for them. She loved them deeply but never spoiled them. I know they deeply miss her. She created the kind of environment that has enabled them to achieve so much in their careers, education and professions. We always talked about them with a lot of pride and gratitude to God. I am glad to mention that her family is one of the best qualified families in Uganda. I sincerely congratulate them.

Until you were told that Rebecca was the Namasole, you would not easily know. Even though she took this role very seriously, our Namasole chose to live a humble life and in that way she was easily accessible to the lay people and won many hearts. She won people's respect and admiration without calling attention to her position.

Thank you very much for this opportunity to write about Rebecca's life; a friend who can never be replaced. I miss her a lot, but I thank God for allowing our paths to cross. I enjoyed the journey with her.

Rebecca thank you for loving me and my family.

NYABO, REST IN PEACE

Mrs. Sarah Mugerwa (Friend)

∞

I met this good friend of mine, Namasole Rebecca Musoke Zirimbuga, in the year 1986, after President Museveni had taken over the Uganda government. We were chosen to be board members on the Resistance Council (RCI) – as it was called then – me as the chairperson, she as the treasurer of the Kyaliwajjala zone. This later became the Local Council (LC).

She did an outstanding job in this position. As you know, all the tasks we had to perform required money. She endeavoured to make sure that every task we began was completed, and she would dig deep into her own pockets to make sure this was done.

In those days, the money that we used we obtained from people who moved into the area. We used to get 1,000 shillings (equivalent to less than 30 cents today) from them. Those who needed letters of recommendation would also give us 1,000 shillings, as well as anyone who needed to have a document notarised; they would give us the same amount. But this was not money coming in daily. We might get one or two of these in a month, whereas the council had many tasks to perform that needed money.

Among the things we did was to convert the underground well-spring that was the town's main water supply into a piped water source. Prior to that, the children collecting water with their jerry cans would step into the water and muddy it. When the money for the project ran out, she completed it with her own money. A time came when we had to train the Local Defence Team (Neighbourhood watch); she paid for that.

Namasole Zirimbuga had sympathy for anyone with a need and she would help them. As a matter of fact, she would fulfil whatever their need was, whether it was a family member, a friend or a stranger. She didn't like talking about anyone behind their back; instead, she would tell people frankly what she thought they were doing wrong and give them her advice. She would never treat anyone spitefully or scornfully.

We took the "Muchaka, Muchaka" (National Service) training together in our Gombolola (sub county) of Kira. Everyone was amazed that she joined in with determination and completed the training without missing a single class. She was always the one who would wake me up early in the morning so that we would not be late.

As the Namasole of Buganda, she was invited to so many kingdom as well private functions. We went to every function she was invited to. She never excused herself saying, "But I just attended such-and-such a function; please accept my apologies." She took on that responsibility without reservation.

Even when they started building the Namasole's palace, she contributed money from her own pocket, although it was someone else's responsibility. When I asked her why she did it, she replied, "We have to do all these things together."

Mrs. Alice Sekagya (Friend)

∞

Mrs. Rebecca Musoke was a very special person indeed. She was a truly caring and loving person and very understanding. She treated us, the Odonga girls who were close friends of her daughters, as her own daughters to such an extent that the Musoke daughters are like blood relatives to us.

I remember how whenever we returned from church (Deliverance Church) a group of us young people would troop to her house at Makerere University, led by her daughter Louise. There would always be food for us kept warm in the oven!

She had a simple faith in God that was very touching. When her husband, Professor Latimer, passed away, she always slept with her bedroom windows open so that the Angels of God could have easy access to her room! To me (Judith (Odonga) Shao) she was a very special person in my life. I do miss her.

I know she is now with her Lord. Thank you Jesus for the life we shared with this wonderful lady: Mukyala Rebecca Latimer Musoke.

Judith (Odonga) Shao (Family friend)

∞

Namasole Rebecca Zirimbuga Musoke was a very good friend of mine. She loved people, she was easy to approach and always empathetic. In her exalted position as the queen mother (Namasole of Buganda) she remained humble and always considerate of those under her responsibility. Among those were the ladies who were caretakers of the Kasubi Tombs.

She was a courageous woman who loved the Kingdom of Buganda. She executed her duties with a sense of commitment and determination, despite her ailing health and she didn't want anyone to know when she was tired. She kept up the work on her dairy farm for so many years, up to the time when the Lord called her home.

She was a strong Christian who loved her God and when we were together in Bible Study Fellowship (BSF) she was always sharing the victories and testimonies of God in her life. She did so much as a woman that you would not have expected from an ordinary person. Truly this Namasole was an exceptional lady and a good example to all of us.

May the Lord truly rest her soul in eternal peace.

Adalina W. Kawesa Lubogo (Friend)

∞

1. Maama Rebecca Musoke Zirimbuga (Namasole) was a true Christian and she loved her church and she loved to pray.

2. She loved to help all types of people, the poor, the rich – she did not discriminate against anyone based on their tribe, their gender or their age.
3. She was a giver, and when she gave you something, it was without reservation and exactly what you would like to make you happy.
4. She was always reluctant to get angry with anyone without telling them the reason why or explaining to them what they did wrong. In the same way, she was quick to forgive.
5. She loved the Kingdom of Buganda and would try her level best to correct anything she felt had gone wrong.
6. She was very humble towards all people with genuine humility.

May you rest in the Lord's eternal peace, Maama.

Victoria Nansubuga (Friend)

∞

1. Maama was a very hardworking lady.
2. Maama was a very gentle lady and she knew how to counsel others wisely so that they could make their own decisions.
3. Maama was a lady who loved to meet the need of anyone who approached her and freely gave money away.
4. Maama was a very friendly person who regularly visited those who were her responsibility. She often travelled abroad to visit her children, but whenever she came back, she would make her rounds visiting her family and friends (in Uganda), especially if you had lost someone while she was away.
5. Another thing I remember about Maama is that she donated all the desks that the children at AUNT MUSOKE NURSERY SCHOOL used to sit on and each desk had her name on it: ZIRIMBUGA NAMASOLE MUSOKE.

6. I, Bob Ssekitoleko, Sunday worked with Maama on her farm when I was still in my youth. I learnt to put up fences, slash grass and destroy anthills in the paddocks. She taught me how to do these things during my holidays while I was still a student looking to earn money for school fees.

7. I grew up with my mother, who Maama Namasole called Ssenga (paternal aunt). Maama advised me to work hard so that I could grow up to be independent and have a place of my own in which to bring up my children - so that after I passed on from this world, I would have something to leave to them. At the time, I thought that was impossible, but with God's help I have managed to do that.

Those are the things I remember about Maama.

Bob Ssekitoleko (Farm manager)

∞

I thank God for the life of Namasole Rebecca Musoke. I thank God for the love that she had for her children and her husband.

I knew Namasole as a lady who believed in educating all of her children, boys and girls. She was always proud of her children's scholastic and career achievements, knowing that she had done all that she could possibly do to give them a good education. I thank her children for continuing to conduct themselves in a manner she would have been proud of.

Namasole was a very hardworking woman. She had a productive vegetable garden as well as a dairy farm that still produces milk today. I used to see her collecting elephant grass and other foodstuffs in her car to feed her cows for many years.

She loved to pray and fast and eagerly supported her church. She was always concerned about how the church would survive and as well as giving support, she would give advice. She encouraged others to support the church as well, and to do God's work without grumbling or complaining.

She was very proud of her heritage, including the legacy of her parents and grandparents who were all committed to their Christian faith. She prayed hard that her children would love God just as much.

Namasole loved her Nkima (Monkey) clan heritage and she often gave money and other material support for the well-being of the clan. She always showed respect for the elders of her clan, even though they were obligated to honour her. She urged Baganda to love their clans, because they are the backbone of the Buganda culture.

Namasole loved the Kingdom of Buganda so much and she gave unreservedly to ensure that the kingdom would survive.

She was always appropriately dressed for the functions she attended in her role as Namasole. She always arrived at the functions before the Kabaka, well-dressed and well-groomed. Keeping time was very important to her and she liked it when other people kept time.

She hated lying and loved the truth. She would say, "Someone who lies can never be trusted." She was an honest person and if she made a pledge, she always fulfilled it. She treated her in-laws with an attitude of both honour and caring.

Time does not allow me to say everything that I would have liked to say, but I thank God for Namasole and I urge her children to make use of the resources she left to them with due diligence. Make sure you know the extent of the land she left you, because she worked so hard to keep it for you, despite the many squatters.

May the Peace of God keep you as you love God, the church, your families, your clans, the Kabaka and the Kingdom of Buganda.

May the Lord be with you all.

Archbishop Livingstone Mpalanyi Nkoyoyo (Retired Archbishop Emeritus, Church of Uganda)

Memories of Mrs. Rebecca Musoke from UK Friends

I first came to Makerere University in April 1972. I was accompanied by my wife, Dorothy, who prior to our marriage in Scotland, had worked as an Administrator in the University of East Africa headquarters and then at Makerere University College.

I was employed as a Lecturer in the recently formed Veterinary School and my primary responsibility was to set up a Clinical Veterinary Service to Livestock Farms. Rebecca and her husband, Professor Musoke, were among my first clients. Rebecca had an excellent well run farm with a herd of good dairy cows. I often visited the farm accompanied by veterinary students under instruction to examine and treat cattle. I remember one day when Rebecca showed me the spring of water on her farm and how it had been maintained by uncleared bush and trees around it. Others had encouraged her to clear away some of the bush but she refused and explained that it was the uncleared bush that was ensuring that the spring would supply a good water output.

At that time in Uganda, "Zero Grazing" of dairy cows became popular and enabled even one good dairy cow to be housed and fed with mainly Napier Grass grown in a small, well-manured, cultivated field and still be productive. However, in the early days of the new scheme, some problems of lameness in the "housed" cows became apparent. I knew how this could be treated, or better still, prevented. I remember Rebecca was so helpful, spending a day with me and coming round some of the farms, helping to get my veterinary advice accepted and telling the farmers of her own experience. I have never forgotten the time she took to help and support me in my work.

Dorothy and I returned to Uganda in 1992 and were so delighted to meet Rebecca again. Later she stayed with us in

Edinburgh, and twice we met her in London with her sister, Damallie. We always delighted in her company, her anecdotes, her good humour and her infectious laughter.

We remained good friends until her untimely death. She was a wonderful person and we both feel greatly privileged to have known her.

David and Dorothy Shannon

∞

My name is Catherine (**Kate**). Damallie has been a valued friend of mine since we were at college together in the 1970s. It was only much later, in fact two years ago, that I met Damallie's beloved sister, Rebecca. It was obvious, way back in our college days, that although she was far from Uganda, Damallie's family were like precious jewels to her and we saw many photos of Mama and Papa, Arnold, Rebecca, Adam and many other family members.

Rebecca had long been a key figure in Damallie's life and they became increasingly close after their parent's passing. I had heard so much about Rebecca from Damallie and was very much looking forward to meeting her when, at last in 2013, I got the chance. We met together for lunch in Denham, along with a mutual college friend and her father. As I walked into the room, Rebecca turned towards me and I thought for a split second "Damallie looks a little different today" and then, of course, I realised the smiling face looking at me was Rebecca's. So alike were they.

I had expected to meet somebody very special and indeed I wasn't disappointed. During our brief encounter, I found her to be a fascinating and charming lady. She had a lively engaging manner and showed interest in all that I had to say. Someone who has the knack of making others feel valued and good about themselves has social skills in abundance. Rebecca was one such person. After lunch we took a short walk through the village and Rebecca told me she was 80 years old. I found that hard to believe because she was such a youthful person.

I have always been proud to say that my college friend is a member of the Ugandan Royal Family. After Rebecca's death, it became obvious to me that she was a very important member of that family. Her loss has no doubt had a big impact on the whole family. Because she had become like a mother figure to Damallie, her death has been sorely felt. I am proud of my friend, Damallie, and proud that I have a link, however tenuous, with the prestigious Kisosonkole family; and fortunate to have met, albeit briefly, with one of its most esteemed and treasured matriarchs. But above all, it is simply the enduring love that Damallie has for her dear sister's memory that is the greatest testament to a very special lady.

∞

I knew Rebecca for a number of years through Damallie. I taught with Damallie at Derwentwater Primary School from 1988 until 1996 and kept in contact with them both when I moved on to become a head teacher. Damallie and Rebecca were very close as sisters, and Damallie made sure Rebecca was always included in parties and gatherings when she visited from Uganda. This is how I got to know Rebecca.

My memories of Rebecca are of a big hearted, cheerful woman who was always interested in other people. Rebecca would take the trouble to ask how things were going in your life. She was genuinely interested in what you had been doing since she last visited and how your family were keeping. What amazed me was her ability to remember everything about the people she met in England, whilst living a busy life in Uganda. Rebecca must have known hundreds of people, yet seemed to be able to remember them all!

When I think of Rebecca, I always remember her smile and sense of fun. She always seemed to enjoy life and could see the funny side of things. I remember her coming to dinner and entertaining us all with tales of Uganda and the people she knew there. Even during her last visit, when she had real difficulty walking and was in pain, she was still the life and soul of the party during the meal we shared at the local Indian Restaurant. She was happy and animated throughout the evening and really seemed to enjoy herself. This was the last time I saw Rebecca and I am glad that I have this happy memory of her to treasure.

Rebecca did have a serious side, and showed real concern for the lives of people in her homeland. I know that she cared deeply about her extended family and the people of Uganda. Rebecca lived through much political change and turmoil during her lifetime and it was always fascinating to hear her talk about the impact of this on herself and others. She held strong opinions about the politics of the country, but was wise enough to know when it was better to say nothing.

In memory of a kind, intelligent, strong, caring woman who lived life to the full and knew the value of laughter.

Anne and Mandy

∞

I cannot recall when I first met Rebecca; it seems as if I have known her for as long as I have known Damallie – and that seems like a lifetime full of great memories. Rebecca was first introduced to me as Damallie's sister, but as I got to know her over the years I could see that she was not only a dear and much loved sister, but also like a mother to Damallie.

Rich and I have reflected together on the person that Rebecca was – kind, loving, incredibly thoughtful and caring. We remember so many times she thanked us for being Damallie's friends and for being there for her when she needed support. There was always a message from Rebecca, whenever Damallie had been home to Uganda or in communication with Rebecca.

We have our photographs to help to recall our memories of Rebecca at social functions at Damallie's house; at our house for parties and other social activities: Rich with his leg in plaster and Rebecca telling me I had to look after him; when I was unwell and Rebecca reminding Rich how he was to look after me; most recently, the Queen's Jubilee Party we held in the garden when it absolutely poured with rain and we had to squeeze everyone into our little living room! Memories of outings over the years to restaurants and on a recent visit for afternoon tea in Kew.

We remember how stalwart Rebecca was when she broke her arm and more recently when she was suffering but without any complaints. We felt that despite living many, many miles away – Rebecca was a good friend and we miss her a great deal. We looked forward to her visits and to catching up; hearing about life in Uganda and telling her all our news. It was a joy to see how close Rebecca and Damallie were.

Memories will continue to come to us of the times we have shared, the conversations we have had and the closeness that we felt to Rebecca. She is missed greatly and much loved.

By Pam and Rich Baker

∞

Rebecca was wonderful Christian lady with a great sense of humour and a love of life. She was strong yet gentle, humble yet proud, interested in everyone yet when you were with her, she made you feel special. She was a woman for all ages, a marvellous example of how to live a life of goodness in the difficult times we find ourselves in today. I believe she has left a legacy of love and service to others through the family she has left here. I thank God that I knew her and that we were able to share good times here in England. Dad joins me in sending this message of love and thanksgiving for a life well lived.

DEREK and MARALYN (MAZ)

∞

I remember Rebecca as a kind, optimistic, considerate and calm yet very strong person. On the few occasions that we spent time together, she always made me feel as if I was her lifelong friend, asking about my health and family and sharing thoughts of her own. I met Rebecca through Damallie, who has been my very good friend for many years and, being the wonderful sister that she was, Rebecca embraced Damallie's friends as if they were her own. She had great dignity and always seemed to be comfortable in every situation she found herself, including having the useful and enviable ability to take catnaps at any time! You would never know what an important position she held in Uganda as she never boasted about it and treated everyone she met with great humility and respect. She was a lovely lady and I am very proud to have known her.

Shirley Ochi

∞

I remember popping round to Damallie's house for something or other, probably work related after school one day about 3 years ago. Rebecca was visiting at the time and she was on the sofa with blankets and jumpers, obviously not enjoying the harsh winter weather! This was the first time I met her. She was ever so friendly to me and I enjoyed listening to her stories about her family who she clearly adored and her farm back in Uganda. At the time, I had just started to date someone new, although I was rather unsure about him mainly as I was living in London and he was a farmer. Our lives couldn't be further apart. Damallie however was excited and we started to talk about when I was next meeting up with him. Rebecca was a very good listener, taking everything in. She was one of those people who really listened; you could tell she was processing everything and when she spoke it was with such wisdom. She said some kind things and some sound advice. She said she thought that he was the one. This struck a chord with me as it was very early days and as I left Damallie's house with Rebecca's words ringing in my ears, couldn't help but smile to myself. Three weeks ago I married this man she described as the one and we are blissfully happy. I like to think that Rebecca not only had a part to play but gave her approval that day.

Gemma Sassoli

∞

It was the night before Rebecca left England for home and I didn't want to miss saying goodbye. I knocked on Damallie's door and went in. However, I could tell that both sisters were a bit sad and down, after all she was leaving the following day. Not being a person to keep the atmosphere miserable, I started to be jolly, joking and cheerful. Very soon Rebecca and Damallie were laughing out loud and behaving like giggling little girls with big smiles on their faces. We were all acting silly. When I left everyone felt a lot more cheerful. That is my memory of Rebecca, a happy laughing lady with a big smile on her face. Sadly missed.

Delia Martland

∞

My memories of Rebecca are very fond ones. She was a truly lovely lady, gracious and kind and always interested in me and my family.

We had many happy meals together and on one occasion she and Damallie came over to spend a Sunday with us. It happened to be Chestnut Sunday in Bushy Park, the park opposite Hampton Court Palace where Henry VIII used to hunt deer. Rebecca was very interested in the idea of a day to celebrate the flowering of the chestnut trees so we decided to join the celebrations. We had to walk a long way and stand for a long time but Rebecca was totally uncomplaining and we had a lovely day.

I will always remember her with great affection.

Sue Buckley

∞

I am very pleased to write about Rebecca. I fondly remember her sweet nature and gentle ways. The two of us would set off to various destinations via tube and bus, whatever the weather. Museums, St. Paul's cathedral, Richmond and an extremely long walk along the South Bank of the Thames. She was a joy to be with, talking endlessly about Buganda and her family. She was interested in everything around us.

We sat by the London Eye drinking coffee; she loved the crowds of people who were queuing to go on it. Then on to Horseguards where she insisted on talking to the sentry on guard and being very amused because he cannot answer.

When I was told she had passed away the memories came flooding back. It was a sad day for me, but to have known her was a joy. She will stay in a corner of my heart forever.

Kit Miller

∞

I first met Rebecca when she came to visit Damallie in London. I had worked with Damallie for many years and knew of her great affection for her sister who was like a mother to her. Usually I met her when we went out for a meal. She proved very good company. She was obviously a very kind and caring person with strong religious beliefs. She was always interested in other people and remembered to ask about their concerns from visit to visit. I was very pleased to invite her to my house when she was suffering from psoriasis and she seemed to enjoy my garden and I certainly enjoyed having her there.

Bozena Chomuick

∞

You asked me for words about Rebecca, Damallie. The words below, remind me of her in the short times that I was in her company. What a gracious lady she was, giving of herself even when feeling the pain of arthritis et al. Her legacy of love and good values grows in you all from her DNA and her example.

These words below are more eloquent than mine and sum Rebecca up well.

Words of E Kubler-Ross:

> The most beautiful people we have known are those who have known defeat, known suffering, known struggle, known loss, and have found their way out of the depths. These persons have a sensitivity and understanding of life that fills them with compassion, gentleness, and a deep loving concern.
>
> BEAUTIFUL PEOPLE DO NOT JUST HAPPEN.
>
> PEOPLE ARE LIKE STAINED GLASS WINDOWS. THEY SPARKLE AND SHINE WHEN THE SUN IS OUT, BUT WHEN THE DARKNESS SETS IN, THEIR TRUE BEAUTY IS REVEALED ONLY IF THERE IS A LIGHT FROM WITHIN.
>
> **Mo Walker**

Lightning Source UK Ltd.
Milton Keynes UK
UKHW012124120521
383626UK00007B/332/J